CAROLS FOR TODAY

JUBILATE HYMNS

EDITOR: MICHAEL PERRY
MUSIC EDITOR: DAVID ILIFF

HODDER AND STOUGHTON
LONDON SYDNEY AUCKLAND TORONTO

Copyright Information

Every effort to trace copyright-holders and to obtain permission has been made; the publishers would welcome details of any errors or omissions, which will be incorporated into future reprints.

British Library Cataloguing in Publication Data

Carols for today: Jubilate Hymns.
   1. Carols, English
   I. Perry, Michael   II. Iliff, David
   783.6′552   M1738

   ISBN 0 340 40317 9

CONTENTS

v

PREFACE

'Glory to God in the highest, on earth peace, goodwill'

Church musicians have two priorities: to aim at competence, and to minister to the congregation. We are to be accurate, attractive, bright – but also reverent, humble . . . and comprehensible. For without understanding there is no response to the word of God. Worse, if the words sung are obscure, trivial, or even foreign to our Christian purpose, then our worship is cynical.

This is no new thought – there are classical statements: Paul insists 'I would rather speak five intelligible words to instruct others than ten thousand words in a tongue'; Cranmer wanted his Divine Service 'understood of the people'. The contexts are different, but the principle is general.

If the shepherds had not been able to understand the angel's message of hope, or the song of glory from heaven, they would not have gone in search of their Saviour. We are to proclaim the good news in word and song so that it is understood and swiftly acted upon. Christmas, now more than ever, is the time for clear speaking and urgency. For the crowds who flock to our churches during the season – a happy and receptive audience – may well not be with us again until next year.

This was the starting point for CAROLS FOR TODAY. We desired to publish good music, the clearest of traditional texts, and contemporary carols which served the double purpose of Christmas worship and Christian teaching.

By these criteria, received texts in other languages required translation – and in most instances, rather than invent new words, we opted for translating material associated with traditional carol tunes. Our group working on carol texts were surprised to find how few modern translations there were. We undertook much of the work ourselves in the spirit of previous editors of hymn and carol books, though on the whole we did not follow the approach of working to initials and pseudonymns. With the notable exception of Timothy Dudley-Smith, whose help and sturdy criticism have been as invaluable as his contributions, contemporary hymn-writers in English have not produced many Christmas carols. As in other carol books, therefore, the editors' work is well represented.

On the music side, there is no slavish reproduction of large numbers of arrangements available in other collections, although many of the best traditional settings are here. Straightforward, singable harmonisations have been provided and, where appropriate, descants, 'last verse in unison' arrangements and choir versions offered. The user will discover in the book the majority of carol tunes in popular use, including some which until now were inapplicable to worship for lack of appropriate words.

The word 'carol' is interpreted not narrowly in terms of a song for Christmas, but in its sense of 'an outpouring of joy'. So the book includes items for Advent and Epiphany too – meeting, we hope, requirements of schools, who break up before Christmas, and churches who go on celebrating afterwards, and of others for whom the services of Christmas itself are the major events of their calendar. In this spirit we have also included some prayers and a wide variety of readings – including our innovative thematic and 'dramatised' readings, with carols carefully cross-referenced to them. To assist selection, the carols are arranged in narrative order – beginning with the promise of the saviour and ending with the recognition 'this is my beloved Son' and our reflection upon the start of the Christian story.

In thankfulness for being allowed to offer our contributions to the Christmas worship of almighty God, and to the proclamation of the good news of Christ's incarnation, we commit this volume to the churches.

MICHAEL PERRY (Editor), Eversley
DAVID ILIFF (Music Editor), Brussels

St Michael and All Angels Day, 1985

PERFORMANCE

Directions for performance (for example tempo, dynamics, harmony or unison) are in many cases minimal as these should be adjusted to suit circumstances. The following points, however, may be helpful:

1 Introductions, where provided, are optional but may be used additionally as an interlude between verses.

2 In a carol with several verses, variety can be obtained by allotting different verses to ladies', girls' and boys', or men's voices.

3 When descants are used, other voices should sing in unison.

PART ONE:
ADVENT

1   O come, O come, Emmanuel

Veni Emmanuel

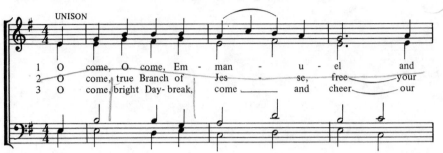

1 O come, O come, Em - man - u - el and
2 O come, true Branch of Jes - se, free your
3 O come, bright Day- break, come and cheer our

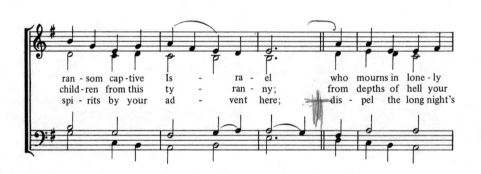

ran - som cap-tive Is - ra - el; who mourns in lone - ly
child-ren from this ty - ran - ny; from depths of hell your
spi - rits by your ad - vent here; dis - pel the long night's

ex - ile here un - til the Son of God draws near:
peo - ple save to rise vic-tor-ious from the grave:
lin - gering gloom and pierce the sha-dows of the tomb:

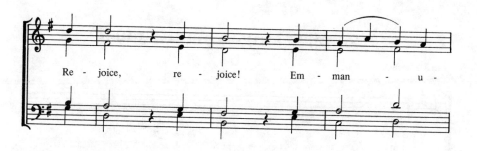

Re - joice,   re - joice!   Em - man - u -

- el shall come to you, O Is - ra - el._____

4 O come, strong Key of David, come
   and open wide our heavenly home;
   make safe the way that leads on high,
   and close the path to misery:
       Rejoice, rejoice!
   Emmanuel shall come to you, O Israel.

5 O come, O come, great Lord of might
   who so long ago on Sinai's height
   gave all your tribes the ancient law,
   in cloud and majesty and awe:
       Rejoice, rejoice!
   Emmanuel shall come to you, O Israel.

Music: from a fifteenth-century French missal
© arranged Noël Tredinnick †

Words: from the Latin (thirteenth century)
J M Neale (1818-1866) and others
© in this version Jubilate Hymns †

2   # Come, O long-expected Jesus

Cross of Jesus

1 Come, O long - ex - pect - ed Je - sus,
2 Is - rael's strength and con - so - la - tion,
3 Born your peo - ple to de - liv - er,
4 By your own e - ter - nal Spi - rit

born to set your peo - ple free!
born sal - va - tion to im - part;
born a child and yet a king;
rule in all our hearts a - lone;

from our fears and sins re - lease us,
dear de - sire of ev - ery na - tion,
born to reign in us for ev - er,
by your all - suf - fi - cient me - rit

Christ in whom our rest shall be.
joy of ev - ery long - ing heart:
now your gra - cious king - dom bring:
raise us to your glo - rious throne.

Music: J Stainer (1840-1901)

Words: C Wesley (1707-1788)
© in this version Jubilate Hymns †

Conditor alme siderum

1 Cre - a - tor of the stars of light, our
2 Through you, the sav - iour cru - ci - fied, the
3 And in the eve - ning of our day you

Lord of mer - cy and of might: O Christ, re - deem - er of us all, with
guilt - y age of death has died; you took our frail hu - man - i - ty and
rose to drive the shades a - way; from Ma - ry's hon-oured vir - gin womb you

fa - vour hear us when we call.
gave the world its re - me - dy.   A - men.
came, to take your peo - ple home.

4 The sun returning to the west,
the moon in pallid splendour dressed,
the glittering stars that pierce the skies,
obedient, keep their boundaries.

5 The unseen worlds below, above,
at your supreme direction move;
soon every creature of your hand
shall bow to your divine command.

6 .We plead with you, our judge and Lord,
to come according to your word;
and in that hour of destiny
to save us from the enemy.

7 Now to the Father, with the Son
and Holy Spirit, Three-in-One;
to God whom heaven and earth adore
be praise and glory evermore! Amen.

This may be sung unaccompanied. If a shorter version is needed, verse *4* and *5* may be omitted.
A standard long metre tune may be used as an alternative.

Music: Mode 4 melody
© arranged John Barnard †

Words: from the Latin
© Michael Perry †

1, 2, 4, 5

4   **Your kingdom come**

Irish

1 Your king - dom come! __ On bend - ed
2 The hours of wait - ing through __ the
3 And there al - rea - dy in __ the
4 The day in whose __ clear shin - ing

knee through pass - ing years __ we pray:
night no less __ to God __ be - long;
skies the dawn's __ first rays __ ap - pear:
light the Lord __ shall stand __ re - vealed,

all __ faith - ful peo - ple long __ to
the __ stars __ de - clare the e - ter - nal
you __ pro - phets of __ our God, __ a -
and __ ev - ery wrong __ be turned __ to

see __ on __ earth __ that king - dom's day.
right __ and __ shame __ the crea - ture's wrong:
- rise, pro - claim the day __ is near:
right, and __ ev - ery hurt __ be healed:

Verse 5 descant

Music: melody from *Hymns and Sacred Poems*, Dublin (1749)
© verse 5 arranged with descant David Nield

Words: F L Hosmer (1840-1929)
© in this version Word & Music †

5   O come, our world's Redeemer

Splendour

1 O come, our world's Redeemer, come! Let every
2 For not by mortal will __ or power, but by the
3 He comes, for whom creation yearns, to face the

age __ a - ston - ished be that God __ should grace the
Ho - ly Spi - rit's breath the seed __ of hea - ven
realms __ of death a - lone; and to __ the Fa - ther

Vir - gin's womb and take our frail __ hu - man - i - ty.
comes to flower, the Word made flesh __ is found __ on earth.
he re - turns to gain a king - dom and __ a throne.

4 He comes to triumph over wrong
and bring us captive back to heaven;
for in our weakness he is strong,
and for his sake we are forgiven.

5 O come, our world's Redeemer, come!
Your manger shines upon our night —
so let the voice of doubt be dumb,
for none shall quench this glorious light!

Music: M Praetorius (1571-1621)

Words: from the Latin
© Michael Perry †

Lift up your heads

6

Gonfalon Royal

UNISON

1 Lift up your heads, you mighty gates;
2 O blessed the land, the city blessed
3 Re - deem - er, come! — we o - pen wide

be - hold, the Lord of glo - ry waits, the
where Christ the ru - ler is con - fessed; the O
our hearts to you this Ad - vent - tide: so

King of kings is draw - ing near, the sav - iour of the
hap - py hearts and hap - py homes to whom this King in
let your Spi - rit guide us on un - til the glo - rious

world is here!
tri - umph comes!
hope is won! A - men.

OR. AT CHRISTMAS

3 Redeemer, come! — we open wide
our hearts to you this Christmastide:
so let your Spirit guide us on
until the glorious hope is won! Amen.

Music: P C Buck (1871-1947)
© Oxford University Press

Words: after G Weissel (1590-1635)
and C Winkworth (1827-1878)
© this version Word & Music †

7   # The Lord will come

St Stephen

1 The Lord will come and not be slow, his
footsteps cannot err; before him righteousness shall go, his royal harbinger.

2 Truth from the earth, like to a flower, shall
bud and blossom then; and justice shall in
heavenly shower come down to us again.

3 Rise, God, and judge the earth in might, its
wicked ways redress; for you are he who
shall by right the nations all possess!

4 The nations all, whom you have made,
shall all your works acclaim,
and come to bow before you, Lord,
and glorify your name.

5 For great you are, and wonders great
by your strong hand are done;
in high and everlasting state
you reign as God alone.

Music: W Jones (1726-1800)

Words: from Psalms 85, 86
J Milton (1608-1674)
© in this version Word & Music †

Take God's good news

8

St Bernard

1 Take God's good news to ____ sad - dened hearts: an
2 The grass shall fade, the ____ flowers shall fall — no
3 Good news for you, Je - ru - sa - lem! good

end to tears there'll be — the glo - ry of the
earth - ly friend is sure; but God has spo - ken
news for lands a - far — the Lord shall come, his

Lord shall shine, and all the world shall ____ see!
and his word shall stand for ev - er - more.
arm shall rule and war shall be no ____ more.

4 The patient Shepherd feeds his flock,
   and gathers every lamb;
   he shields them all,
      the Mighty One,
   and keeps his sheep from harm.

5 How blessed the heralds
      of good news
   who spread God's word of peace;
   who sing aloud
      the Saviour's name,
   'The Lord our Righteousness':

6 From mountain-top let voices ring,
   'In Christ, our God has come —
   to share our life, to bear our grief,
   to bring us safely home!'

Music: *Tochter Zion*, Cologne (1741)

Words: from Isaiah 40
© David Mowbray †

9   **You servants of the Lord**

Narenza

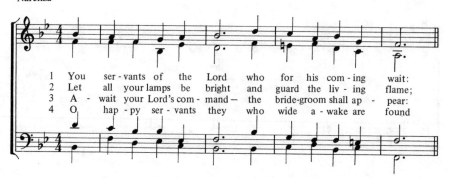

1 You ser - vants of the Lord who for his com - ing wait:
2 Let all your lamps be bright and guard the liv - ing flame;
3 A - wait your Lord's com - mand— the bride-groom shall ap - pear:
4 O hap - py ser - vants they who wide a - wake are found

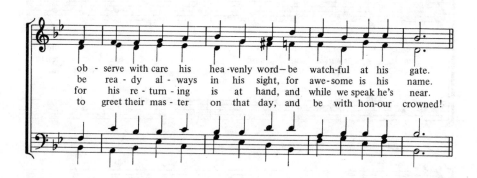

ob - serve with care his hea - venly word— be watch-ful at his gate.
be rea - dy al - ways in his sight, for awe-some is his name.
for his re - turn - ing is at hand, and while we speak he's near.
to greet their mas - ter on that day, and be with hon-our crowned!

DESCANT

5 Christ shall the ban - quet spread with

MELODY

5 Christ shall the ban - quet spread with

PIANO
or
ORGAN

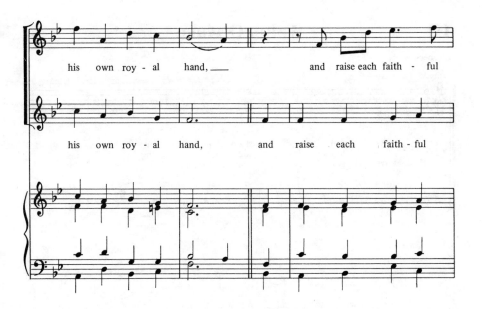

his own roy - al hand, ____ and raise each faith - ful

his own roy - al hand, and raise each faith - ful

ser - vant's head a - mid the an - gel - ic band.

ser - vant's head a - mid the an - gel - ic band.

Music: adapted from J Leisentritt
Catholicum Hymnologium (1584)
arranged by W H Havergal (1793-1870)
© verse 5 arranged with descant John Barnard †

Words: from Luke 12
P Doddridge (1702-1751)
© in this version Word & Music †

10   Wake, O wake

Sleepers, wake

1 Wake, O wake, and sleep no longer,
for he who calls you is no stran - ger:
a - wake, God's own Je - ru - sa - lem! Hear the
mid - night bells are chim - ing the sig - nal

2 Zi - on hears the sound of sing - ing;
her heart is thrilled with sud - den long - ing:
she stirs, and wakes, and stands pre - pared. Christ her
friend, and lord, and lov - er, her star and

3 Glo - ry, glo - ry, sing the an - gels,
while mu - sic sounds from strings and cym - bals:
all hu - man - kind, with songs a - rise! Twelve the
gates in - to the ci - ty, each one a

for _ his   roy - al _____ com - - - ing: let _ voice _ to _
sun _ and   strong re - deem - - - er –   at _ last _____ his _
pearl _ of   shin - ing _____ beau - - - ty;   the _ streets _ of _

voice _ an - nounce _ his   name!   We   feel _ his _ foot - step _
might - y   voice _ is   heard.   The   Son _ of _ God _ has _
gold _ ring out _____ with praise.   All   crea - tures _ round _ the _

near,   the _ Bride - groom at _____ the _ door –   Al - le -
come   to _ make _____ with us _____ his _ home: sing _ Ho -
throne   a - dore _____ the   ho - ly _____ One   with _ re -

- lu - - ia!   The   lamps _ will _ shine with _ light _ di -
- san - - na!   The   fight _ is _____ won,   the _ feast _ be -
- joi - - cing: A - men _ be _____ sung by _____ ev - ery

- vine   as _____ Christ _ the _____ sav - iour   comes _ to   reign.
- gun;   we _____ fix _____ our _____ eyes _____ on   Christ _ a - lone.
tongue   to _____ crown _ their _ wel - come   to _____ the   King. ·

Music: P Nicolai (1556-1608)
arranged J S Bach (1685-1750)

Words: after P Nicolai (1556-1608)
© Christopher Idle †

11

Lo, he comes

Helmsley

DESCANT

4 Yea, let all a - dore thee,

1 Lo, he comes with clouds de - scend - ing,
2 Ev - ery eye shall now be - hold him
3 The dear to - kens of his pas - sion
4 Yea, a - men, let all a - dore thee,

high on thine e - ter - nal throne; Sav - iour, take the

once for fa - voured sin - ners slain; thou - sand thou - sand
robed in dread - ful ma - je - sty; those who set at
still his dazz - ling bo - dy bears, cause of end - less
high on thine e - ter - nal throne; Sav - iour, take the

power and glo - ry, claim the king - dom

saints at - ten - ding swell the tri - umph
naught and sold him, pierced and nailed him
ex - ul - ta - tion to his ran - somed
power and glo - ry, claim the king - dom

for thine own: Al - le - lu -

of __ his __ train: __ Al - le - lu - ia,
to __ the __ tree, __ deep - ly wail - ing,
wor - ship - pers: __ with __ what rap - ture,
for __ thine __ own: __ Al - le - lu - ia,

- ia, al - le - lu - ia, al - le - lu - ia!

al - le - lu - ia, al - le - lu - ia!
deep - ly wail - ing, deep - ly wail - ing,
with __ what rap - ture, with __ what rap - ture,
al - le - lu - ia, al - le - lu - ia!

e - ver - last - ing God, __ come down!

God ap - pears, on earth __ to __ reign.
shall the __ true Mes - si - ah __ see.
gaze we __ on those glor - ious __ scars!
e - ver - last - ing God, __ come __ down!

Music: eighteenth-century English melody
© descant David Iliff †

Words: after J Cennick (1718-1755)
C Wesley (1707-1788) and
M Madan (1726-1790)

12   Hark! a trumpet call

Merton

DESCANT

5 Hon - our, glo - ry, might and bless - ing

1 Hark! a trum - pet call is ___ sound - ing,
2 Wak - ened by the so - lemn __ warn - ing,
3 See! the Lamb, so long ex - pec - ted,

to the Fa - ther and the Son, with the ev - er -

'Christ is near,' it seems to __ say: 'Cast a - way the
let the earth - bound soul a - rise; Christ, her __ sun, all
comes with par - don down from _ heaven; let us __ haste, with

- last - ing __ Spi - rit, while __ e - ter - nal a - ges run!

dreams of dark - ness, child - ren of the dawn - ing __ day!'
harm dis - pel - ling, shines up - on the morn - ing __ skies.
tears of sor - row, one and all to be for - given:

4 That, when next he comes in glory
and the world is wrapped in fear,
with his mercy he may shield us,
and with words of love draw near.

5 Honour, glory, might and blessing
to the Father, and the Son,
with the everlasting Spirit,
while eternal ages run!

Music: W H Monk (1823-1889)
© descant John Barnard †

Words: from the Latin (sixth century)
E Caswall (1814-1878)

Besançon Carol

D.C. for v3

nou - rish, that ___ in time ___ the flower ___ may

Look   east,   peo - ple, look

Look ___   east,   look ___

flou - rish. Peo - ple, look   east,   and   sing   to -

___   Look ___   east,   and   sing   to -

east —   Love   is   on   the   way.

east —   Love   is   on   the   way.

- day —   Love,   the   Rose,   is   on ___ the   way.

- day ___   Love   is   on   the   way.

4 An-gels, an-nounce to man and beast:— he is com-ing from— the east; set ev-ery peak and val-ley hum-ming with — the word:— the Lord— is com-ing! Peo-ple, look east, and sing— to-day — Love, the Lord, is on — the way.

A simpler arrangement of this tune (with other words) appears at number 34.

Music: French traditional melody
© arranged Barry Rose

Words: Eleanor Farjeon (1881-1965)
© Oxford University Press

Hark the glad sound

Bristol

DESCANT

4 Our glad ho - san - nas, ___ Prince ___ of ___ peace, your

1 Hark the glad sound! — the Sav - iour comes, the
2 He comes the pri - soners to re - lease in
3 He comes the bro - ken heart to bind, the
4 Our glad ho - san - nas, Prince of peace, your

wel - come ___ shall pro - claim; and heaven's e - ter - nal

Sav - iour ___ pro - mised long; let ev - ery heart pre -
Sa - tan's ___ bond - age held; the gates of brass be -
wound - ed ___ soul to cure; and with the trea - sures
wel - come ___ shall pro - claim; and heaven's e - ter - nal

arch - es ___ ring with your be - lov - ed name.

- pare a ___ throne and ev - ery voice a ___ song.
- fore him ___ burst, the ir - on fet - ters ___ yield.
of his ___ grace to en - rich the hum - ble ___ poor.
arch - es ___ ring with your be - lov - ed ___ name.

Music: Ravenscroft's *Psalter* (1621)
© descant David Iliff †

Words: P Doddridge (1702-1751)

15 Jesus the saviour comes

Little Cornard

1 Jesus the saviour comes! ___ Greet him with joy - ful song,
   prince of the hea - venly throne, ___ pro - mised to earth so long: he
   comes to fight our mor - tal foe and car - ry all our sin and woe.

2 Jesus the saviour comes! ___ Lord o - ver life and death;
   sin and de - struc - tion die, ___ felled by his ho - ly breath: tri -
   - um-phant from the cross and grave he comes to heal and bless and save.

3 Jesus the saviour comes! ___ sove - reign and Lord of all;
   na - tions, do - min - ions, powers — all at his feet must fall: he
   comes to ban - ish death and sin and bring his hea-venly king - dom in.

4 Lord of the Christmas crib,
  Lord of the cross of shame,
  humbly we worship you,
  proudly we take your name:
  be all our joy till advent drums
  and trumpets cry, 'The saviour comes!'

5 Then with your ransomed hosts,
  faultless before your face,
  sons of the living God,
  born of redeeming grace,
  your love we'll sing, your power we'll praise:
  your name adore through endless days!

Music: M Shaw (1875-1958)
© J Curwen and Sons Limited
Sole selling agents William Elkin Music Services

Words: © 1983 Margaret Clarkson

We hail the approaching God

16

St Thomas

4 Soon, shining in the cloud,
 the Lord will come again
 and take his Body to the skies
 to live and love and reign.

5 Then night and death shall yield,
 and sin be done away;
 then Adam shall be made anew
 on that tremendous day.

6 To Father, Spirit, Son,
 the God whom we adore,
 be highest praise and honour now,
 and glory evermore!

Music: A Williams' *New Universal Psalmodist* (1770)
© descant John Barnard †

Words: after C Coffin (1676-1749)
© Michael Perry †

17   Jesus — hope of every nation

Halton Holgate

1 Je - sus — hope of ev - ery na - tion, light of heaven up -
2 Men of faith on God de - pend - ing wait to see Mes -
3 Look, he comes! the long - a - wait - ed Christ, re - deem - er,
4 Glo - ry in the high - est hea - ven to the Fa - ther,

- on our way; pro - mise of the
- si - ah born; sin's op - press - ive
liv - ing Word; hope and faith are
Spi - rit, Son; and on earth let

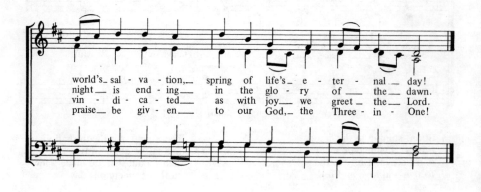

world's sal - va - tion, spring of life's e - ter - nal day!
night is end - ing in the glo - ry of the dawn.
vin - di - ca - ted as with joy we greet the Lord.
praise be giv - en to our God, the Three - in - One!

Music: later form of melody by W Boyce (1711-1779)
arranged mainly S S Wesley (1810-1876)

Words: from Luke 2
The Song of Simeon/Nunc dimittis
© Michael Perry †

Joy to the world

Antioch

1 Joy to the world! The Lord has come: let earth re-ceive her king, let ev-ery heart pre-pare him room and heaven and na-ture sing, and heaven and na-ture sing, and heaven, and heaven and na-ture sing! and heaven and na-ture sing!

2 Joy to the earth! The sav-iour reigns: your sweet-est songs em-ploy, while fields and streams and hills and plains re-peat the sound-ing joy, re-peat the sound-ing joy, re-peat, re-peat the sound-ing joy. re-peat the sound-ing joy.

3 He rules the world with truth and grace, and makes the na-tions prove the glo-ries of his right-eous-ness, the won-ders of his love, the won-ders of his love, won-ders, won-ders of his love. the won-ders of his love.

Music: L Mason (1792-1872), based on a theme by G F Handel (1685-1759)

Words: I Watts (1674-1748)

19   # Christ is the Truth

The Truth from above

1 Christ is the Truth sent from a - bove, the
2 Though God had given us all things good, yet
3 For at this sea - son of the year our
4 Thus he in love to us be - haved, and

Truth of God, the God of love: there -
sin we did and sin we would; though
blessed re - deem - er did ap - pear; he
showed us how we must be saved; to

- fore don't turn him from your door, but
we were heirs to death and hell, God
came to serve and came to teach, and
free us from our mor - tal pain, he

hear him all, both rich and poor.
sent his Son with us to dwell.
ma - ny thou - sands and heard him preach.
lived and died and rose a - gain.

Music: English traditional melody
arranged by R Vaughan Williams (1872-1958)
© arrangement Stainer & Bell Ltd

Words: traditional, collected by E M Leather
and R Vaughan Williams (1872-1958)
© Stainer & Bell Ltd,
in this version Word & Music †
by permission of Mrs Leather

The people who in darkness walked 20

Dundee

1 The people who in darkness walked have
2 To greet you, Sun of righteousness, the
3 For now to us a child is born, to

seen a glorious light: that light shines out on
ga - thering na - tions come; re - joic - ing as when
us a son is given; and on his shoul - der

those who lived in sha - dows of the night.
reap - ers bring their har - vest trea - sures home.
ev - er rests all power in earth and heaven.

4 His name shall be the prince of peace,
eternally adored;
most wonderful of counsellors,
the great and mighty Lord.

5 His peace and righteous government
shall over all extend;
on judgement and on justice based,
his reign shall never end.

Music: *Scottish Psalter*, Edinburgh (1615)

Words: from Isaiah 9
J Morison (1750-1798)
© in this version Jubilate Hymns †

21 The darkness turns to dawn
(Saigon)

Saigon

1 The darkness turns to dawn, the
2 The Son of God most high, be -
3 God's Word of truth and grace made

day-spring shines from heaven; for un - to us a
-fore all else be - gan, a vir - gin's son be -
flesh with us to dwell; the bright - ness of the

child is born, to us a Son is given.
-hold him lie, the new - born Son of Man.
Fa - ther's face, the child Em - man - u - el.

4 How rich his heavenly home!
How poor his human birth!
As mortal man he stoops to come,
the light and life of earth.

5 A servant's form, a slave,
the Lord consents to share;
our sin and shame,
our cross and grave,
he bows himself to bear.

6 Obedient and alone
upon that cross to die —
and then to share
the Father's throne
in majesty on high.

7 And still God sheds abroad
that love so strong to send
a saviour, who is Christ the Lord,
whose reign shall never end.

The darkness turns to dawn

(Sandys)

22

Sandys

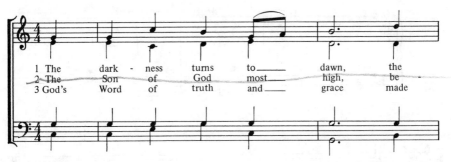

1 The dark - ness turns to dawn, the
2 The Son of God most high, be
3 God's Word of truth and grace made

day - spring shines from heaven; for un - to us a
- fore all else be - gan, a vir - gin's son be -
flesh with us to dwell; the bright - ness of the

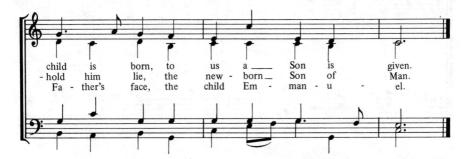

child is born, to us a Son is given.
- hold him lie, the new - born Son of Man.
Fa - ther's face, the child Em - man - u - el.

4 How rich his heavenly home!
How poor his human birth!
As mortal man he stoops to come,
the light and life of earth.

5 A servant's form, a slave,
the Lord consents to share;
our sin and shame,
    our cross and grave,
he bows himself to bear.

6 Obedient and alone
upon that cross to die—
and then to share
    the Father's throne
in majesty on high.

7 And still God sheds abroad
that love so strong to send
a saviour, who is Christ the Lord,
whose reign shall never end.

Music: English traditional melody
from W Sandys' *Christmas Carols* (1833)

Words: © Timothy Dudley-Smith

23

Bow down, you stars

Sibford Gower

ORGAN

1 Bow down, you stars_____ and moon and sun!_____
2 You mea-sured years,_____ and hours and days,_____
3 Lift up your heads,_____ you sons of earth!_____

the Source of all your light____ is come;____
fill ev - ery mo - ment with____ his____ praise:____
your great Cre - a - tor comes____ to____ birth;____

the fire that burns____ with - in his heart____
for he who knows____ no time or space____
and with a ba - by's lone - ly cry,____

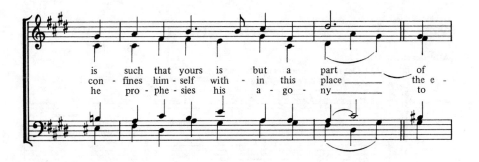

is   such that yours is   but   a   part _____ of
con - fines him - self with - in   this place _____ the e -
he   pro - phe - sies   his   a - go - ny _____ to

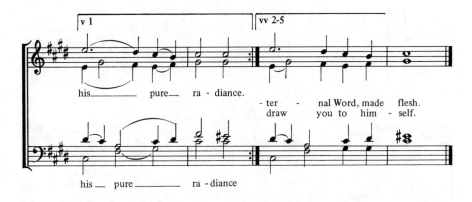

v 1
his ____ pure ___ ra - diance.

vv 2-5
-ter - nal Word, made flesh.
draw   you to   him - self.

his __ pure _____ ra - diance

4 No thrilling music with its spell,
  no artist's brush, or pen can tell
  the yearning love, consuming care
  that brings you to that manger bare —
      our Lord, Emmanuel.

5 Lord Jesus, Saviour, mighty King,
  our lives, our all, to you we bring;
  for by that lowly path you trod,
  you loved us back to you, our God —
      to make us heirs of heaven!

A tender shoot

A tender shoot

Andante tranquillo ma non troppo

SOPRANO
1 A ten - der shoot has start - ed
2 This shoot, I - sai - ah taught us, from

ALTO
1 A ten - der shoot has start - ed
2 This shoot, I - sai - ah taught us, from

TENOR
1 A ten - der shoot has start - ed
2 This shoot, I - sai - ah taught us, from

BASS
1 A ten - der shoot has start - ed
2 This shoot, I - sai - ah taught us,

sempre p
up from a root of grace, as an - cient seers im -
Jes - se's root should spring; the vir - gin Mar - y

sempre p
up from a root of grace, as an - cient seers im -
Je - se's root should spring; the vir - gin Mar - y

sempre p
up from a root of grace, as an - cient seers im -
Jes - se's root should spring; the vir - gin Mar - y

as an - cient seers im -
the vir - gin Mar - y

p
- part - ed from Jes - se's ho - ly race; it
brought us the branch of which we sing: our

p
- part - ed from Jes - se's ho - ly race; it
brought us the branch of which we sing: our

p
- part - ed from Jes - se's ho - ly race; it
brought us the branch of which we sing: our

p
- part - ed from Jes - se's ho - ly race; it
brought us the branch of which we sing: our

Music: O Goldschmidt (1829-1907)
© collected 1964 Gamut Distribution

Words: O Goldschmidt (1829-1907)
translated W Bartholomew
© collected 1964 Gamut Distribution

Gabriel the angel came

Angelus ad virginem

PIANO
or
ORGAN

mp

1 Ga - bri - el the an - gel came to greet the vir - gin
2 Ma - ry asked, 'How can it be: my love is given to
3 Ma - ry then with joy re - plied 'I serve the Lord of

Ma - ry: 'Peace!' he said, and called her name, 'For
no - one, Jo - seph is be - trothed to me — can
hea - ven: God shall be my hope and guide — to

joy - ful news I car - ry: the Lord of
what is done be un - done?' 'The Spi - rit
him my heart is giv - en who low - ly

all from realms a - bove has looked up -
comes — and this is how God's power will
stoops to fill my cup and raise his

on your soul___ in love; you___ shall give birth to
be up-on___ you now: Don't___ be a-fraid, what
hum-ble ser-vant up. God's___ will this day I

Christ on earth,___ the Sav - iour; you
God has said___ will cheer___ you — the
shall o - bey___ re - joic - ing: then

bear the hope___ of grace — the___ mark of hea - ven's
pro - mise is___ not vain — all___ peo - ple shall___ re -
let the na - tions sing, such___ love and mer - cy

fa - vour, and all shall see___ God's face.'
-vere___ you, and vir - tue shall___ re - main.'
voic - ing, and praise their Lord___ and king!'

Music: fourteenth-century English melody
© arranged John Barnard †

Words: from the Latin
© Michael Perry †

26   # When the angel came to Mary

Sans Day Carol

1 When the an - gel came to Ma - ry he ___
2 When the an - gel came to Ma - ry he ___
3 When the an - gel came to Ma - ry he ___
4 When the an - gel came to Ma - ry, she ___

said, ___ 'Be at peace, for the Lord God shall be
said, ___ 'Do not fear, for his power shall be up -
said, ___ 'Hear his name, for his ti - tle shall be
said, ___ 'Be it so: for the Lord God is my

with ___ you, his ___ love will not cease.'
on ___ you, a ___ child you will bear.' And ___
Je - sus of ___ king - ly ac - claim.'
mas - ter, his ___ will I must do.'

Ma - ry bore___ Je - sus Christ, our___ sav - iour for to

be; ___ and the first___ and the___ last ___ and the___

great - est is he, is he, is he; and the

first and the___ last___ and the___ great - est is he.

Music: Cornish traditional melody
© arranged John Barnard †

Words: from the traditional carol
© in this version Word & Music †

27   The angel Gabriel

Gabriel's Message

1 The an-gel Ga-bri-el from hea-ven came,____ his
2 'Fear not, for you shall bear a ho-ly child,____ by
3 Then gen-tle Ma-ry hum-bly bowed her head:____ 'To

wings as drift-ed snow, his eyes as as flame:____
him shall man to God be re-con-ciled,____
me be as it plea-ses God,' she she said,____

'From God, all hail' the an-gel said to Ma-ry,____ 'most
his name shall be Em-man-u-el, the long-fore-told:__ most
'My soul shall praise and mag-ni-fy his ho-ly name.'__ Most

high-ly fa-voured la-dy!' Glo - ri - a! ____
high-ly fa-voured la-dy!' Glo - ri - a! ____
high-ly fa-voured la-dy! Glo - ri - a! ____

4 'And so,' she said, 'how happy I shall be!
  All generations will remember me,
  for God has kept the promises to Israel.'
    Most highly favoured lady!
    Gloria!

5 Of her, Emmanuel — the Christ — was born
  in Bethlehem, upon that Christmas morn.
  And Christian folk throughout the world will ever say,
    'Most highly favoured lady!
    Gloria!'

Music: Basque Noël
arranged C E Pettman (1866-1943)
© 1961 H Freeman
Reproduced by permission of EMI Music Publishing Ltd
and International Music Publications

Words: S Baring-Gould (1834-1924)
© in this version Word & Music †

My soul proclaims

Andrew Mark

Flowing (♩ = 100)

UNISON

1 My soul pro-claims the great-ness of the Lord,_____ and my
2 In ev-ery age, for those who fear the Lord_____ come his
3 To Is-ra-el his ser-vant he brings help,_____ and the

spi-rit sings for joy to my sa-viour God!_____ His
mer-cy, and the strength of his migh-ty arm:_____ he
pro-mise to our fa-thers is now ful-filled:_____ for

low-ly slave he looked up-on in love:_____ they will
routs the proud, throws mon-archs off their thrones,_____ while he
Christ has come ac-cord-ing to his word,_____ and the

call me hap-py now, for migh-ty are the works he has
lifts the low-ly high, fills hun-gry souls with food, and the
mer-cy that he showed to A-bra-ham is now for his

done, and ho-ly is his name!_____
rich sends em-pty a-way._____
child-ren's child-ren ev-er-more._____

v 3

Music: © Norman Warren †

Words: from Luke 1
The Song of Mary/Magnificat
© Christopher Idle †

29   Now sing, my soul

Bitterne

1 Now sing, my soul, 'How great the Lord!'— re-
2 For ev - er af - ter, I'll be known as
3 Through - out all a - ges, those who fear his

- joice, my spi - rit, in your God: my sav - iour who has
hap - piest of the hu - man race; the might - y One has
ma - je - sty, shall know his grace; his power-ful works dis -

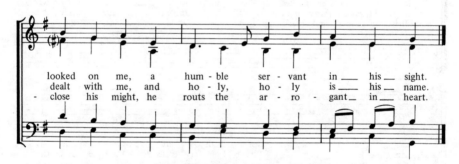

looked on me, a hum - ble ser - vant in his sight.
dealt with me, and ho - ly, ho - ly is his name.
- close his might, he routs the ar - ro - gant in heart.

4 From thrones great rulers have been torn,
 yet humble folk are raised on high;
 the hungry have been satisfied,
 the wealthy, he shall turn away.

5 To Israel, servant of the Lord,
 comes yet again the promised hope:
 in Abraham and all his line,
 God's mercy ever shall endure.

6 Give glory then to God above,
 give praise to Christ his only Son;
 give thanks for all the Spirit's power,
 both now and through eternity!

Words: from Luke I
The Song of Mary/Magnificat
© Michael Saward †

Music: © Brian Bailey †

As Joseph was awaking

(Cherry Tree Carol)

Cherry Tree Carol

1 As Jo - seph was a - wak - ing he ___
2 And nei - ther was he born ___ in ___
3 And nei - ther was he cov - ered in ___

heard ___ an ___ an - gel ___ sing, 'There shall be born to
house ___ nor ___ yet in ___ hall; nor in the place of
fi - ne - ry so ___ fair, but in such hum - ble

Ma - ry on ___ earth our hea - venly King.'
par - a - dise, but ___ in an ox - 's stall.
cloth - ing as ___ all the ba - bies wear.

4 And neither was he cradled
   in silver nor in gold,
   but in a wooden manger
   to keep him from the cold.

5 As Joseph was awaking
   he heard an angel sing,
   'There shall be born to Mary
   on earth our heavenly King.'

Music: English traditional melody

Words: English traditional
© in this version Word & Music †

31 As Joseph was awaking

Joseph

(Joseph)

As Jo-seph was a-wak-ing he heard an an-gel sing,____

'There shall be born to Ma-ry on earth our hea-venly King.'____

1 And nei-ther was he born____ in house nor yet in hall;____
2 And nei-ther was he cov-ered in fi-ne-ry so fair,____
3 And nei-ther was he cra-dled in sil-ver nor in gold,____

nor in the place of pa-ra-dise, but in an ox-'s
but in such hum-ble cloth-ing as all the ba-bies
but in a wood-en man-ger to keep him from the

stall.____
wear.____ Now-ell,____ now-ell!
cold.____

Music: R R Terry (1865-1938)
© J Curwen and Sons Limited
Sole selling agents William Elkin Music Services

Words: English traditional
© in this version Word & Music †

PART TWO:
CHRISTMAS

To Bethlehem the strangers came 32

Stranger in Bethlehem

1 To Beth - le - hem the stran - gers came from all the coun - try
2 To Beth - le - hem the stran - gers came, sweet Ma - ry and her
3 To Beth - le - hem a Stran - ger came from far be - yond the

round, and un - a - ware that God was there they fell to sleep - ing
man, no room to spare, no com - fort where a ho - ly life be -
earth; he came to share his Fa - ther's care, to bring us se - cond

sound:
- gan: Stran - ger in Beth - le - hem to whom the an - gels
birth:

sing; man - ger in Beth - le - hem, cra - dle for a king!

33   **A virgin most holy**

A virgin most pure

1 A __ vir - gin most __ ho - ly __ as pro - phets do
2 At __ Beth - le - hem __ Ju - dah, a ci - ty re -
3 But __ when __ they __ had __ en - tered the ci - ty so
4 Then __ were __ they __ ob - liged in a sta - ble to

tell — has __ brought __ forth __ a __ ba - by a -
- nowned, both __ Ma - ry __ and __ Jo - seph — his
fair, they __ could __ not __ get __ shel - ter, for
sleep, where __ tra - vel - lers __ hor - ses and

- mong us to dwell, to be our re - deem - er from __
par - ents-were found; they came to be __ count - ed, with __
ma - ny were there; and Jo - seph and __ Ma - ry, whose __
don - keys did keep; they had there poor __ com - fort and __

death __ and __ from __ sin, which A - dam's __ trans -
o - ther __ folk __ too, as __ Cae - sar __ Au -
sub - stance __ was __ small, could __ find __ at __ the __
slept __ on __ the __ hay, but __ Ma - ry __ bore __

-gress - ion had___ caught us all___ in.
-gus - tus had___ said they should_ do.
inn___ there no___ lodg - ing at___ all.
Je - sus, our___ sav - iour, next_ day. And___

there - fore___ be___ mer - ry — re - joice and be___

mer - ry, make___ mu - sic___ and___ sing, for___

Je - sus___ our___ sav - iour is___ born_ to be___ king!

Music: English traditional melody
arranged C Wood (1866-1926)

34

Mary, ride on

Besançon Carol

PIANO
or
ORGAN

1 Ma - ry, ride on to Da - vid's town, Beth - le -
2 Shep - herds, come see in Da - vid's town, shep - herd
3 An - gels, pro - claim to Da - vid's town Je - sus

-hem with glo - ry crown; bear your child to bear our
of the world come down; see your sav - iour, see your
Christ of high re - nown! Son of Man and king of

weep - ing, rock him wa - king, rock him sleep - ing.
heal - ing, wor - ship hum - bly, wor - ship knee - ling. Al - le -
glo - ry, here to tell sal - va - tion's sto - ry.

- lu - ia! Sing this night: Christ is born, e - ter - nal light!

A more elaborate arrangement of this tune (with other words) appears at number 13.
Music: French traditional melody
© arranged John Barnard †

Words: © Paul Wigmore †

Child in a stable

Dans cette étable

1 Child in a sta - ble: how love - ly is this place where God is a - ble to show such per - fect grace! No prince-ly babe that smiled or pa - lace that be - guiled, in his - to - ry or fa - ble, could ev - er match this child with - in a sta - ble.

2 God comes in weak - ness, and to our world for love de - scends with meek - ness from realms of light a - bove. This Child shall heal our wrong, for sor - row give a song, and hope in place of bleak - ness; for no-thing is so strong as God in weak - ness.

3 Now night is end - ed! the cha - sm that di - vides at last is mend - ed, and God with us a - bides. For on this hap - py morn new glo - ry wakes the dawn; the Sun is high a - scen - ded — to us a Child is born, and night is end - ed!

Music: French traditional melody
© arranged John Barnard †

Words: after E Flèchier (1632-1710)
© Michael Perry †

36 A stable lamp

Dayton

1 A sta - ble lamp is
2 This child through Da - vid's
3 Yet he shall be for -
4 But now, as at the

light - ed whose glow shall wake the sky; the
ci - ty shall ride in tri -umph by; the
- sak - en, and yield - ed up to die; the
end - ing, the low is lift - ed high; the

stars shall bend their voic - es, and ev - ery stone shall
palm shall strew its branch - es, and ev - ery stone shall
sky shall groan and dark - en, and ev - ery stone shall
stars shall bend their voic - es, and ev - ery stone shall

Music: E Routley (1917-1982)
© 1976 Hinshaw Music, Inc

Words: from *Advice to a prophet*
Richard Wilbur
© Faber and Faber Limited

37 Come, see a little tender babe
(Newtown Linford)

Newtown Linford

1 Come, see a lit-tle ten-der babe, in freez-ing win-ter night, who in a man-ger tremb-ling lies, a sad and sor-ry sight. 2 The
3 Des-pise him not for ly-ing there; first, what he is en-quire: an or-ient pearl is of-ten found in depths of dir-ty mire. 4 Judge
5 This sta-ble is a prin-ce's court, this crib his chair of state; the beasts are part of all his pomp, the dish his roy-al plate. 6 The
7 With joy ap-proach, O Christ-ian soul, do hom-age to your king; and high-ly praise his hum-ble birth, and of his glo-ry sing!

vv 1, 3, 5   v 7   Fine.

2 inns are full, and none will give̲̲̲̲̲ this lit - tle pil - grim
4 not his crib, his wood-en dish, nor beasts that by him
6 per - sons in that poor at - tire his roy - al liv - eries

bed, but forced is he a - mong the beasts in crib to
feed; judge not his mo-ther's poor at - tire, nor Jo-seph's
wear; the Prince him-self has come from heaven — such pomp is

D.C.

shroud his head.
man - ner heed.
val - ued there.

D.C.

Music: © Peter White †

Words: R Southwell (1561-1595)
© in this version Word & Music †

38   Come, see a little tender babe

(Peak Hill)

Peak Hill

1 Come, see a lit - tle ten - der babe, in freez - ing win - ter night,___ who in a man - ger trem - bling lies, a sad and sor - ry sight. ___ 2 The inns are full and none will give this lit - tle pil - grim bed, ___ but

3 Des - pise him not___ for ly - ing there; first, what he is en - quire: ___ an or - ient pearl ___ is of - ten found in depths of dir - ty mire. ___ 4 Judge not his crib, his wood - en dish, nor beasts that by ___ him feed; ___ judge

5 This sta - ble is ___ a prin - ce's court, this crib his chair of state; ___ the beasts are part ___ of all his pomp, the dish his roy - al plate. ___ 6 The per - sons in that poor at - tire his roy - al liv - eries wear; ___ the

forced is he — a - mong the beasts in crib to shroud his head.—
not his mo - ther's poor at - tire, nor Jo - seph's man - ner heed.—
Prince him - self — has come from heaven— such pomp is val - ued

there. — 7 With joy ap - proach, O Christ - ian soul, do

hom - age to — your king; — and high - ly praise — his

hum - ble birth, and of his glo - ry sing! —

Music: © Norman Warren †

Words: R Southwell (1561-1595)
© in this version Word & Music †

39   O little town of Bethlehem
(Forest Green)

Forest Green

1 O lit-tle town of _ Beth-le-hem, how still we _ see you _ lie!
2 For Christ is born of _ Ma - ry and, ga - thered all a - bove
3 How si - lent-ly, how_ si - lent-ly the won-drous gift is _ given!
4 O ho - ly child of _ Beth-le - hem, de-scend to _ us, we _ pray;

A - bove your deep and_ dream-less_sleep, the si - lent_ stars go _ by:
while mor-tals sleep, the_ an - gels_keep their watch of _ won - dering_ love:
So God im-parts to_ hu - man_hearts the bless-ings_ of his_heaven:
cast out our sin and_ en - ter _ in, be born in_ us to - day!

yet_ in your dark_ streets_ shin - ing is _ ev-er - last - ing_ light;
O _ morn-ing stars, to - ge - ther pro - claim the ho - ly _ birth,
no _ ear may hear _ his _ co - ming, but _ in this world of _ sin,
We _ hear the Christ-mas _ an - gels the _ great glad tid - ings_ tell —

the _ hopes and fears of_ all _ the_years are met in_you to - night.
and _ prai - ses sing to_ God_ the_ king, and peace to_ all the _ earth.
where meek souls will re - ceive_ him - still_ the dear Christ_ en - ters_ in.
O _ come to us, a - bide_ with_ us, our Lord Em - man - u - el.

Music: English traditional melody
arranged R Vaughan Williams (1872-1958)
© arrangement Oxford University Press

Words: P Brooks (1835-1893)

O little town of Bethlehem

40

(Christmas Carol)

Christmas Carol

1 O lit-tle town of Beth-le-hem, how still we see you lie!
2 For Christ is born of Ma-ry and, ga-thered all a-bove
3 How si-lent-ly, how si-lent-ly the won-drous gift is given!
4 O ho-ly child of Beth-le-hem, de-scend to us, we pray;

A-bove your deep and dream-less sleep the si-lent stars go by;
while mor-tals sleep, the an-gels keep their watch of won-dering love:
So God im-parts to hu-man hearts the bless-ings of his heaven:
cast out our sin and en-ter in, be born in us to-day!

yet in your dark streets shin-ing is ev-er-last-ing light;
O morn-ing stars, to-ge-ther pro-claim the ho-ly birth,
no ear may hear his com-ing, but in this world of sin.
We hear the Christ-mas an-gels the great glad tid-ings tell —

the hopes and fears of all the years are met in you to-night.
and prai-ses sing to God the king, and peace to all the earth.
where meek souls will re-ceive him — still the dear Christ en-ters in.
O come to us, a-bide with us, our Lord Em-man-u-el.

Music: H Walford Davies (1869-1941)
© Oxford University Press

Words: P Brooks (1835-1893)

41   Once in royal David's city

Irby

1 Once in roy-al Da-vid's ci - ty stood a low-ly cat - tle
2 He came down to earth from hea - ven who is God and Lord of
3 And through all his won-drous child-hood he would hon-our and o -

shed, where a mo - ther laid her ba - by in a
all; and his shel - ter was a sta - ble and his
- bey, love and watch the gen - tle mo - ther in whose

man - ger for his bed: Ma - ry was that mo - ther
cra - dle was a stall: with the poor and meek and
ten - der arms he lay: Christ - ian child-ren all should

mild, Je - sus Christ, her lit - tle child.
low - ly lived on earth our sa - viour ho - ly.
be kind, o - be - dient, good as he.

4 For he is our childhood's pattern:
  day by day like us he grew;
  he was little, weak and helpless;
  tears and smiles like us he knew:
  and he feels for all our sadness,
  and he shares in all our gladness.

5 And our eyes at last shall see him,
  through his own redeeming love;
  for that child, so dear and gentle,
  is our Lord in heaven above;
  and he leads his children on
  to the place where he has gone.

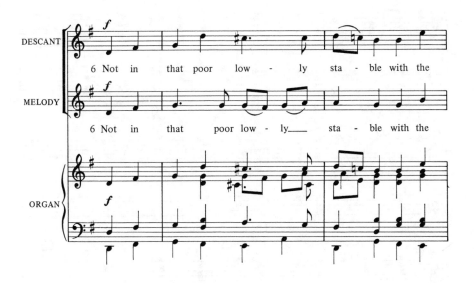

see_ him, but in hea - ven, set at God's_ right hand on

see him, but_ in_ hea - ven, set at God's right hand_ on_

ff

high: there _____ his ___ child - ren ga - ther ___

ff

high: there his child - ren ga - ther

ff

allarg.

round bright _____ like ___ stars,_ with_ glo - ry____ crowned.

round bright like stars, with glo - ry____ crowned.

allarg.

Music: H J Gauntlett (1805-1876)
arranged A H Mann (1850-1929)
© verse 6 arranged with descant Paul Edwards †

Words: C F Alexander (1818-1895)

In the bleak mid-winter

Cranham

1 In the bleak mid - win - ter frost - y wind made moan, ___ earth stood hard as ir - on, wa - ter like a stone; snow had fall - en, snow on snow, snow ___ on ___ snow, in the bleak mid - win - ter long ___ a - go.

2 Hea - ven can - not hold him, nor ___ earth sus - tain; ___ heaven and earth shall flee a - way when he comes to reign: in the bleak mid - win - ter a sta - ble place suf - ficed God, the Lord al - migh - ty, Je - sus ___ Christ.

3 En - ough for him whom cher-u - bim wor - ship night and day ___ a breast - ful of milk and a man-ger full of hay; e - nough for him whom an - gels fall ___ down be - fore, the wise men and the shep - herds who ___ a - dore!

4 What ___ can I give him, poor ___ as I am? ___ If I were a shep - herd I would give a lamb, if I were a wise ___ man I would do my part; yet what I can I give him — give ___ my ___ heart.

Music: G Holst (1874-1934) Words: C G Rossetti (1830-1894)

43 Child of heaven

Il est né

Child of hea-ven born on earth— let the— mu-sic— sound his prais-es;

Child of hea-ven— born on earth— sing to greet the— sav-iour's birth!

1 Christ, our hope, our— joy, ap-pears — for this— time we— have been wait-ing;
2 Cold with-in a— low-ly cave — tight-ly— wrapped, in— man-ger ly-ing;
3 Je-sus, king and— might-y one, gen-tle— babe in— Ma-ry's keep-ing;

Christ, our hope, our joy, ap - pears — pro-mise of a thou - sand years.
cold with - in a low - ly cave is our God who stoops to save.
Je - sus, king and might - y one, come to make our hearts your throne!

Last time

Child of hea - ven born on earth — let the mu - sic sound his prais - es;

Child of hea - ven born on earth — sing to greet the

sav - iour's birth! molto rall.

Music: French traditional melody
© arranged John Barnard †

Words: from the French
© Michael Perry †

44
Not in lordly state

Rhuddlan

1 Not in lord - ly state and splen - dour, loft - y pomp and
2 His no rich and sto - ried man - sion, king - ly rule and
3 Yet the eye of faith be - holds him, King a - bove all
4 Not in lord - ly state and splen - dour, loft - y pomp and

high re - nown;—— in - fant - form his robe most roy - al,
scep - tred sway;—— from his seat in high - est hea - ven
earth - ly kings;—— Lord of un - cre - a - ted a - ges,
high re - nown;—— in - fant - form his robe most roy - al,

lant - ern - light his on - ly crown; see the new - born—
throned a - mong the beasts— he lay: see the new - born—
he whose praise e - ter - nal rings — see the new - born—
lan - tern - light his on - ly crown; Christ the new - born—

King of glo - ry,—— Lord of all to earth come down!
King of glo - ry — cra - dled in his couch of hay!
King of glo - ry — pan - o - plied by an - gels' wings!
King of glo - ry,—— Lord of all to earth come down!

Music: Welsh traditional melody
from *Musical Relicks of the Welsh Bards* (1800)

Words: © Timothy Dudley-Smith

Child in the manger

Bunessan

UNISON

1 Child in the man - ger, in - fant of Ma - ry,
2 Once the most ho - ly child of sal - va - tion
3 Pro - phets fore - told him, in - fant of won - der;

out - cast and stran - ger, Lord of all!
gen - tle and low - ly lived be - low:
an - gels be - hold him on his throne:

child who in - her - its all our trans - gres - sions,
now as our glo - rious might - y re - deem - er,
worth - y our sav - iour of all their prais - es;

all our de - mer - its on him fall.
see him vic - tor - ious o - ver each foe.
hap - py for ev - er are his own.

Music: Gaelic melody
© arranged Noël Tredinnick †

Words: after M MacDonald (1789-1872)
L Macbean (1853-1931)

46   Child of the stable's secret birth

(Morwenstow)

Morwenstow

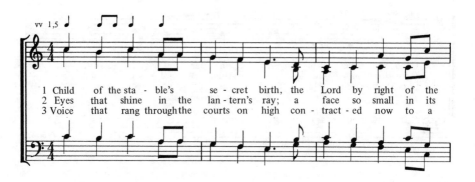

vv 1,5

1 Child of the sta - ble's se - cret birth, the Lord by right of the
2 Eyes that shine in the lan - tern's ray; a face so small in its
3 Voice that rang through the courts on high con - tract - ed now to a

vv 2,4

lords of earth, let an - gels sing of a king new - born, the
nest of hay, face of a child, who is born to__ scan __the
word - less cry, a voice to mas - ter the wind and__ wave, the

omit in v 5

world is weav - ing a crown of thorn: a crown of thorn for that
world he made through the eyes of man: and from that face in the
hu - man heart and the hun - gry grave: the voice of God through the

in - fant head   cra - dled soft in the man - ger bed.
fin - al day   earth and heaven shall   flee   a - way.
ce - dar trees   rol - ling forth as the sound of seas.

4 Infant hands in a mother's hand,
  for none but Mary may understand
  whose are the hands and the fingers curled
  but his who fashioned and made our world:
  and through these hands in the hour of death
  nails shall strike to the wood beneath.

5 Child of the stable's secret birth,
  the Father's gift to a wayward earth,
  to drain the cup in a few short years
  of all our sorrows, our sins and tears —
  ours the prize for the road he trod:
  risen with Christ; at peace with God.

Music: Christopher Dearnley
© Oxford University Press

Words: © Timothy Dudley-Smith

47   Child of the stable's secret birth

Secret Birth

(Secret Birth)

1 Child of the sta - ble's se - cret birth, the Lord by right of the lords of earth, let an - gels sing of a king new - born, the world is weav - ing a crown of thorn:

2 Eyes that shine in the lan - tern's ray; a face so small in its nest of hay, face of a child who is born to scan the world he made through the eyes of man:

3 Voice that rang through the courts on high con - tract - ed now to a word - less cry, a voice to mas - ter the wind and wave, the hu - man heart and the hun - gry grave:

a crown of thorn for that in - fant head
and from that face in the fin - al day
the voice of God through the ce - dar trees

cra - dled soft in the man - ger bed.
earth and hea - ven shall flee a - way.
rol - ling forth as the sound of seas.

4 Infant hands in a mother's hand,
  for none but Mary may understand
  whose are the hands and the fingers curled
  but his who fashioned and made our world:
  and through these hands in the hour of death
  nails shall strike to the wood beneath.

5 Child of the stable's secret birth,
  the Father's gift to a wayward earth,
  to drain the cup in a few short years
  of all our sorrows, our sins and tears —
  ours the prize for the road he trod:
  risen with Christ; at peace with God.

48   Mary had a baby — sweet lamb

Mary had a baby

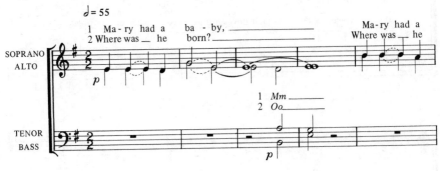

Music: West Indian traditional melody
© arranged John Barnard †

Words: traditional

49

Mary had a baby, yes, Lord

Mary had a baby

1 Ma - ry had a ba - by, yes, Lord; _
QUESTION 2 What _ did she name him, yes, Lord; _
ANSWER 3 Ma - ry named him Je - sus, yes, Lord; _

Ma - ry had a ba - by, yes, my Lord; Ma - ry had a ba - by,
what _ did she name him, yes, my Lord; what _ did she name him,
Ma - ry named him Je - sus, yes, my Lord; Ma - ry named him Je - sus,

yes, Lord! The peo - ple keep a - com-ing but the train has gone!
yes, Lord? Or
yes, Lord! The peo - ple keep a - com-ing for to see her child!

QUESTION:

4 Where was he born,
  yes, Lord..?

QUESTION:

6 Where did she lay him,
  yes, Lord..?

ANSWER:

5 Born in a stable,
  yes, Lord..!

ANSWER:

7 Laid him in a manger,
  yes, Lord..!

Music: West Indian traditional melody
© arranged David Iliff †

Words: © in this version Word & Music †

Donkey and ox

Entre le boeuf et l'âne gris

UNISON

1 Don - key and ox a - round his bed,
2 Ma - ry's the arms a - round him held,
3 Li - ly and rose a - round him spread,
4 There, on this glad and ho - ly day,

sleeps, sleeps, sleeps the lit - tle Boy:
sleeps, sleeps, sleeps the lit - tle Boy:
sleeps, sleeps, sleeps the lit - tle Boy:
sleeps, sleeps, sleeps the lit - tle Boy:

An - gel hosts re - joice, thou-sands with one voice

sing - ing praise a - bove to this God of love.

A more elaborate arrangement of this carol appears on the next page.

Music: French traditional melody
© arranged John Barnard †

Words: from the French
© Paul Wigmore †

51 Donkey and ox
(Choir arrangement)

Entre le boeuf et l'âne gris

Music: French traditional melody
© arranged John Barnard †

Words: from the French
© Paul Wigmore †

52   Christ is born for us today

Resonet in laudibus (ii)

UNISON

1 Christ is born for us to-day — rough the man - ger,
2 Child of grace at Ma - ry's knee, he is born to
3 Christ - ians all, re - joice and sing with the com - ing

soft the hay; all who will con - fess him may re -
set us free; he is born our hope to be, our
of our King; let the bells of hea - ven ring to

- ceive the Son, the ho - ly One of Ma - ry.
God, our Lord, by all a - dored for ev - er.
tell the earth of Je - sus' birth to Ma - ry!

Another arrangement of this tune, but with refrain, appears at number 74.

Music: fourteenth-century German melody
© arranged David Iliff †

Words: J M Neale (1818-1866)
© in this version Word & Music †

Within this humble manger 53

Vom Himmel hoch

mp With - in__ this hum - ble__ man - ger lies the__
Lord__ who__ reigns a - bove __ the __ skies;
with - in the__ stall__ where__ beasts __ have__ fed, the__
vir - gin - born__ lays__ down__ his__ head.

Organ

Music: from *Christmas Oratorio*
J S Bach (1685-1750)

Words: from the German
J Troutbeck (1832-1899)

I see your crib

I see your crib

SOPRANO

1 I see your crib — a cra - dle where the cat - tle cry, __

__ and in the stall you lie, sweet Ma - ry's ho - ly boy. The

pro - mise, and the love, God gives — yet in the world a -

- round no place for him is found. __ 'No room!' they

cried — our Lord was left out - side. __

SOPRANO

2 I see your face, so full __ of

ALTO

2 I see your face, so full __ of

love   in   sleep ⸺   and   shep - herds   leave   their   sheep   to

love   in   sleep ⸺   and   shep - herds   leave   their   sheep   to

mf

come   and   wor - ship   here.   Good   news, which choirs   of

come ⸺   and ⸺   wor - ship   here.   *mf*   Good

an   -   gels   tell: God's   on - ly,   won - drous

news   they   tell: God's   on - ly,   won - drous

Son   to   us   on   earth has   come. ⸺   See   where he   lies   in

Son   to   us   on   earth has   come. ⸺

> *p*

straw;   gaze,   wor - ship, and   a - dore! ⸺

p

gaze,   wor - ship, and ⸺   a - dore! ⸺

3 I see your star — a guide, the way for men and kings, the gift of God who brings sal - va - tion from our sins, to grow in grace with God and man.__ He had no home, no bed: 'Come, fol - low me!' he said ___ Lord, let me hear your call, and bring my life,__ my__ all! ___

Holy child
(Ruxley)

Ruxley

1 Ho - ly child, — how still __ you lie! safe __ the
2 Ho - ly child, — whose birth - day brings __ shep - herds
3 Ho - ly child, — what gift __ of grace from __ the

man - ger, soft __ the hay; __ faint __ up - on __ the
from __ their field __ and fold, __ an - gel choirs __ and
Fa - ther free - ly willed! __ In __ your in - fant

east - ern sky __ breaks __ the dawn __ of Christ - mas Day.
east - ern kings, __ myrrh __ and frank - in - cense __ and gold:
form __ we trace __ all __ God's pro - mis - es __ ful - filled.

4 Holy child, whose human years
span like ours delight and pain;
one in human joys and tears,
one in all but sin and stain:

5 Holy child, so far from home,
all the lost to seek and save:
to what dreadful death you come,
to what dark and silent grave!

6 Holy child, before whose name
powers of darkness faint and fall;
conquered, death and sin and shame —
Jesus Christ is Lord of all!

7 Holy child, how still you lie!
safe the manger, soft the hay;
clear upon the eastern sky
breaks the dawn of Christmas Day.

Music: © Brian Hoare †

Words: © Timothy Dudley-Smith

56 Holy child

Holy child

1 Ho-ly child, ———— how still you lie! safe the
3 Ho-ly child, ———— what gift of grace from the
5 Ho-ly child, ———— so far from home, all the
7 Ho-ly child, ———— how still you lie! safe the

man - ger, soft the hay; faint up - on ———— the east - ern
Fa - ther free - ly willed! In your in - fant form we
lost to seek and save, to what dread - ful death you
man - ger, soft the hay; clear up - on ———— the east - ern

sky breaks the dawn of Christ - mas Day.
trace all God's pro - mis - es ful - filled.
come, to what dark and si - lent grave!
sky breaks the dawn of Christ - mas Day.

2 Ho - ly child, _____ whose birth - day brings _____ shep - herds
4 Ho - ly child, _____ whose hu - man years _____ span like
6 Ho - ly child, _____ be - fore whose name _____ powers of

from their field and fold, an - gel choirs and east - ern
ours de - light and pain; one in hu - man joys and
dark - ness faint and fall; con - quered, death and sin and

kings, myrrh and frank - in - cense and gold:
tears, one in all but sin and stain:
shame — Je - sus Christ is Lord of all! _____

v6

Music: © Michael Baughen †
© arranged David Iliff †

Words: © Timothy Dudley-Smith

57 Away in a manger

Cradle Song

DESCANT

Ah _____ Ah _____

1 A - way in a __ man-ger, no __ crib for a bed, the __ lit - tle __ Lord
2 The cat - tle are __ low-ing, the __ ba - by a - wakes, but __ lit - tle __ Lord
3 Be near me, Lord __ Je - sus; I __ ask you to stay close __ by me for

Ah _____

Je - sus laid __ down his sweet head; the stars in the __ bright sky looked
Je - sus __ no __ cry - ing he makes: I love you, Lord __ Je - sus __ look __
e - ver and __ love me, I pray; bless all the dear __ child-ren in __

Ah _____

down where he lay __ the __ lit - tle __ Lord Je - sus a - sleep on the hay.
down from __ on high and __ stay by __ my side un - til __ morn-ing is nigh.
your ten - der care, and __ fit us __ for hea-ven to __ live with you there.

If the descant is not used then the version opposite in a higher key may be considered more suitable.

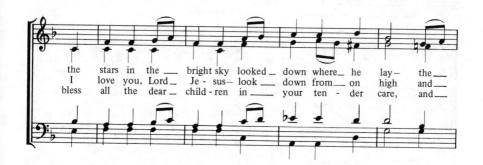

1 A - way in a ___ man - ger, no ___ crib for a bed, the ___
2 The cat - tle are ___ low - ing, the ___ ba - by a - wakes, but ___
3 Be near me, Lord ___ Je - sus; I ___ ask you to stay ___ close ___

lit - tle ___ Lord Je - sus laid ___ down his sweet head;
lit - tle ___ Lord Je - sus ─ no ___ cry - ing he makes:
by me ___ for ev - er and ___ love me, I pray;

the stars in the ___ bright sky looked ___ down where ___ he lay ─ the ___
I love you, Lord ___ Je - sus ─ look ___ down from ___ on high and ___
bless all the dear ___ child - ren in ___ your ten - der care, and ___

lit - tle ___ Lord Je - sus a - sleep on the hay.
stay by ___ my side un - til ___ morn - ing is nigh.
fit us ___ for hea - ven to ___ live with you there.

Music: W J Kirkpatrick (1838-1921)
© arranged with descant John Barnard †

Words: verses 1, 2 unknown (nineteenth century)
verse 3 J T McFarland (c 1906)

58   **Sing lullaby**

The infant King

1 Sing lul - la - by! lul - la - by ba - by, now re - clin - ing: sing lul - la - by! Hush, do not wake the in - fant king; an - gels are watch - ing, stars are shin - ing o - ver the place where he is ly - ing: sing lul - la - by.

2 Sing lul - la - by! lul - la - by ba - by, sweet - ly sleep - ing: sing lul - la - by! Hush, do not wake the in - fant king; soon will come sor - row with the morn - ing, soon will come bit - ter grief and weep - ing: sing lul - la - by!

3 Sing lul - la - by! lul - la - by ba - by, gen - tly doz - ing: sing lul - la - by! Hush, do not wake the in - fant king; soon come the cross, the nails, the pierc - ing, then in the grave at last re - pos - ing: sing lul - la - by!

4 Sing lul - la - by! lul - la - by! Is the baby wak - ing? sing lul - la - by! Hush, do not stir the in - fant king, dream - ing of Eas - ter, joy - ful morn - ing, con - quer - ing death, its bond - age break - ing: sing lul - la - by!

Music: Basque noël
arranged C E Pettman (1866-1943)
© arrangement 1954 H Freeman and Co.
Reproduced by permission of EMI Music Publishing Limited
and International Music Publications

Words: S Baring-Gould (1834-1924)

O slumber, heaven-born treasure 59

Schlaf wohl

1 O slumber, heaven-born trea-sure, now— sleep soft - ly, ho - ly child, — as
2 For Ma - ry, with— her lov-ing hands has laid you down_to sleep, — while
3 When you are grown_you shall be great — but then comes Cal - va - ry, _____ where

shep - herds poor_ be - fore you bow,—on whom the an - gel smiled: _ with
Jo - seph by — your cra - dle stands_his faith - ful watch_ to keep; ___ there
men shall seize_ you in their hate__and nail you to ___ a tree: ___ but

ten - der love_they join ___ to sing _ a lul - la - by_ to hea - ven's king. __
on the straw the ox - en mild _ are ly - ing still—sleep ho - ly child! _
sweet-est dreams be yours to-night—sleep ho - ly child_till morn-ing light!_

Lul - la - by, ___ lul - la - by, _____ sleep, sleep soft - ly, lul - la - by.

Music: K Leuner
© arranged David Iliff †

Words: from the German
J Davies (1787-1855)
© in this version Word & Music †

60   Sleep, Lord Jesus

Dormi Jesu

1 Sleep,__ Lord__ Je - sus!__ Ma - ry__ smi - ling __ on__ her__

in - fant__ so be - guil - ing sings__ a__ joy - ful__

lul - la - by.__ 2 Sleep,__ Lord__ Je - sus!__ Ma - ry__

griev - ing __ at __ the __ fate __ our__ sin __ is weav - ing __

sings __ a __ so - lemn __ lul - la - by. 3 Sleep, __ Lord __

Je - sus! __ Ma - ry __ dream - ing __ of __ this __ fal - len __

world's re - deem - ing sings __ a __ ho - ly __ lul - la -

- by. __ Sleep, __ Lord __ Je - sus, __ lul - la - by!

61

I saw my love

O Waly Waly

1 I saw my love by lan-tern light, my new-born child so frail and — fair, and through the — toils of that long — night I saw my love all lone-ly ___ there.

2 I saw my love by morn-ing light, this ho-ly boy, so sweet and — fair, and in his — eyes I saw the — sight of all the earth in an-guish — there.

3 I saw my love by noon-day light, the King of love, so strong and — fair, and in his — hands I saw the — might of all the powers of hea-ven ___ there.

4 I saw my love by evening light,
the sinner's friend, so young and fair,
and in his death I saw no fright
but life eternal springing there.

5 I saw my love by lantern light,
my newborn child so frail and fair,
and through the toils of that long night
I saw my love all loving there.

Music: English traditional melody
© arranged Noël Tredinnick †

Words: © Paul Wigmore †

The daylight is fading

62

Es wird scho glei dumpa

1 The day-light is fa - ding, the eve - ning is
2 The star-light is com - ing — the dawn - ing of

near: O Child in the man - ger, there's noth - ing to
pain, the an - guish, the sor - row for souls to re -

fear; I'll stand by your cra - dle this ho - ly night
- gain: but an - gels bring — joy — to your Beth - le - hem

long, I'll sing to you soft - ly — so sleep to my
night — no pa - lace was lit — by such hea - ven - ly

song, lit - tle Child, lit - tle Child, so — sleep to my song!
light, lit - tle Child, lit - tle Child, so — sleep to my song!

A more elaborate arrangement, for two part singing, appears on the next page.

Music: Tyrolean melody
© arranged John Barnard †

Words: © Paul Wigmore †

63

The daylight is fading
(Choir arrangement)

Es wird scho glei dumpa

day - light is fa - ding, the eve - ning is near: O

Child in the man - ger, there's no - thing to fear; I'll

stand by your cra - dle this ho - ly night long, I'll

*See note at the end of this arrangement.

sing   to   you   soft - ly —   so   sleep   to   my   song: lit - tle

Child,   lit - tle   Child,   so __ sleep   to   my   song!

poco rall.   a tempo

p

2 The

mp

2 The   star - light   is

pa - lace was lit __ by such hea - ven - ly light, lit - tle Child, so __

lit __ by such hea - ven - ly light, lit -tle Child, lit - tle Child, so __

rall.　　a tempo

sleep to my song!

sleep to my song!

rall.　　a tempo　　　　　　rall.

This arrangement may be used for unison singing, in which case the lower part alone should be used in verse 2.

If mixed voices are available, it is suggested that the treble voices sing verse 1 and take the upper part in verse 2, the men singing the lower part.

If the two-part version is to be sung by treble voices only, the number of singers allocated to the upper part should be about one third of the total.

An arrangement for four part singing appears at number 62.

Music: Tyrolean melody
© arranged John Barnard †

Words: © Paul Wigmore †

64   ## Jesus, saviour, holy child

Rocking

1 Je - sus, sav - iour, ho - ly___ child, sleep to - night,
2 From your Fa - ther's home you___ come to this___ earth,
3 Now to hea - ven's glo - ry___ song we re - ply

slum - ber___ deep till ___ morn - ing___ light. Lul - la - by, our
by your___ low - ly___ man - ger___ birth! Child of God, our
with a ___ Christ - mas ___ lul - la - by. Hush, the e - ter - nal

joy, our trea - sure, all our hope and all our plea - sure: at the cra - dle
na - ture shar - ing; Son of Man, our sor - rows bear - ing; rich, yet here a -
Lord is sleep - ing close in Ma - ry's ten - der keep - ing: babe on whom the

where you ___ lie we will ___ wor - ship:___ Lul - la - by!
- mong the ___ poor: Christ the ___ Lord, whom we a - dore!
an - gels ___ smiled – Je sus, ___ sav - iour, ho - ly___ child.

Music: Moravian melody
© arranged David Iliff †

Words: © Michael Perry †

O Jesus my Lord

65

O Jesulein süss

1 O Jesus my Lord, how sweetly you lie so far from home in heaven on high: you come to do the Father's will, to feel our pain, to cure our ill, to live and serve, to love and die!

2 O Jesus my Lord, how sweetly you lie— a helpless babe in poverty: you deign to share our earthly fate, and by your grace illuminate the valley of our misery!

3 O Jesus my Lord, how sweetly you lie— the Son revealed to human eye: so light in us your flame of love that we may lift our hearts above to him whom angels glorify!

4 O Jesus my Lord, how sweetly you lie and show us God's humility: accept the offering at our hands of faithfulness to your commands, and praise throughout eternity!

Music: German melody in Scheidt's *Tabulaturbuch* (1650)
arranged J S Bach (1685-1750)

Words: after S Scheidt (1587-1654)
© Michael Perry †

Descend from heaven

Susanni

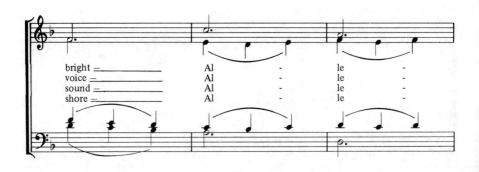

1 De - scend ___ from heaven, you an - gels
2 Come, greet ___ our world with tune - ful
3 So let ___ your cheer - ful mu - sic
4 Sing, 'Peace, ___ good - will from shore ___ to

bright ___ Al - le -
voice ___ Al - le -
sound ___ Al - le -
shore ___ Al - le -

- lu - ia; Lul - la - by, lul - la - by,
- lu - ia; Lul - la - by, lul - la - by,
- lu - ia; Lul - la - by, lul - la - by,
- lu - ia; Lul - la - by, lul - la - by,

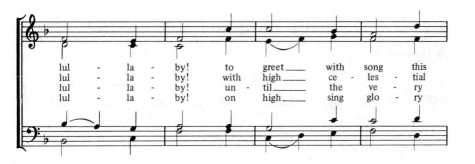

lul - la - by! to greet____ with song this
lul - la - by! with high____ ce - les - tial
lul - la - by! un - til____ the ve - ry
lul - la - by! on high____ sing glo - ry

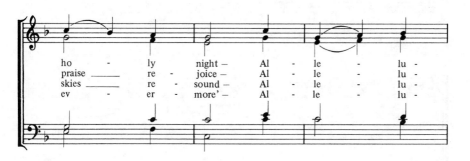

ho - ly night — Al - le - lu -
praise ____ re - joice — Al - le - lu -
skies ____ re - sound — Al - le - lu -
ev - er - more' — Al - le - lu -

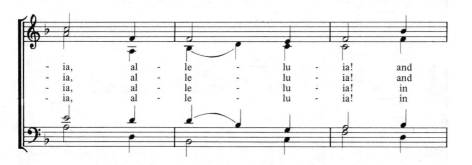

- ia, al - le - lu - ia! and
- ia, al - le - lu - ia! and
- ia, al - le - lu - ia! in
- ia, al - le - lu - ia! in

tell ____ of Je - sus, Ma - ry's Son.
tell ____ of Je - sus, Ma - ry's Son.
praise ____ of Je - sus, Ma - ry's Son.
praise ____ of Je - sus, Ma - ry's Son.

Music: German traditional melody
© arranged David Iliff †

Words: G R Woodward (1848-1934)
© in this version Word & Music †

67 I heard a mother tenderly sing

Old Basque Noël

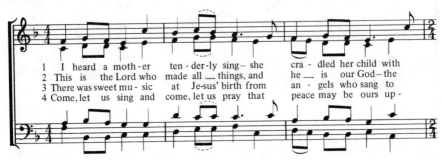

1 I heard a moth-er ten-der-ly sing— she cra-dled her child with
2 This is the Lord who made all __ things, and he __ is our God—the
3 There was sweet mu-sic at Je-sus' birth from an-gels who sang to
4 Come, let us sing and come, let us pray that peace may be ours up-

gen-tle rock - ing:
King of all kings. Lul - lay, _____ lul - lay, _____ my __
greet the whole earth.
- on this glad day.

dear __ son, my sweet __ one; lul - lay, _____ lul -

- lay, __ my __ dear son, my __ own __ dear dar - ling!

Music: arranged C E Pettman (1866-1943)
© arrangement 1961 H Freeman and Co.
Reproduced by permission of EMI Music Publishing Limited
and International Music Publications

Words: fifteenth century
© in this version Word & Music †

Glad music fills the Christmas sky   68

Deus tuorum militum

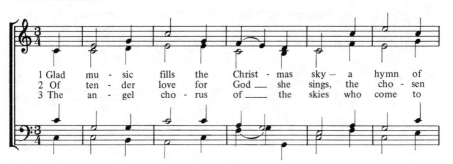

1 Glad mu - sic fills the Christ - mas sky — a hymn of
2 Of ten - der love for God __ she sings, the cho - sen
3 The an - gel cho - rus of __ the skies who come to

praise, __ a song of love; the an - gels wor - ship
Mo - ther of the Son; she knows _ that won - ders
tell __ us of God's grace have yet __ to know his

high __ a - bove and Ma - ry sings _ her lul - la - by.
have _. be - gun, and trusts _ for all __ the fu - ture brings.
hu - man face, to watch _ him die, __ to see him rise.

4 Let praise be true and love sincere,
rejoice to greet the saviour's birth:
let peace and honour fill the earth
and mercy reign — for God is here!

5 Then lift your hearts and voices high,
sing once again the Christmas song:
for love and praise to Christ belong —
in shouts of joy, and lullaby.

Music: Grenoble *Antiphoner* 1753
© arranged David Iliff †

Words: © Michael Perry †

69 Travellers all to Bethlehem

Geborn ist uns ein Kindelein

PIANO
or
ORGAN

1 Tra - vel - lers all ____ to Beth - le -
2 Beau - ti - ful child ____ up - on ____ my
3 Shep - herd - boy, with ____ your eyes ____ so
4 Tra - vel - lers from ____ the East ____ come

- hem, they sing ____ for me ____ and
breast, of all ____ my songs ____ I'll
bright to see ____ a king ____ by
down to find ____ this king ____ with -

I ____ for them; the song ____ they sing ____ is
sing ____ the best; my lul - la - by ____ this
lan - tern - light, let your ____ sweet voice ____ with
- out ____ a crown! The crown ____ he'll wear ____ no

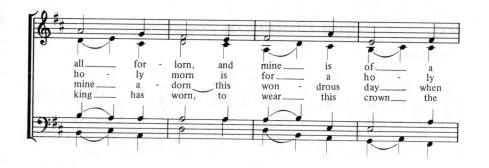

all____ for - lorn, and mine____ is of____ a
ho - ly morn is for____ a ho - ly
mine____ a - dorn this won - drous day____ when
king____ has worn, to wear____ this crown____ the

ba - by born:
sav - iour born:
Christ ____ is born: O hear _____ the
Christ ____ is born.

song____ I sing ____ to - day ____ that

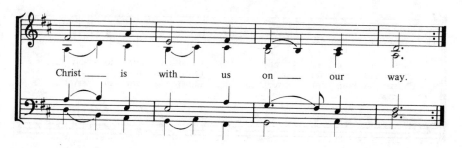

Christ ____ is with____ us on ____ our way.

Music: fifteenth-century melody
from J Spangenberg (1484-1550)
© arranged David Iliff †

Words: © Paul Wigmore †

70   Good Christians all, rejoice

In dulci jubilo

1 Good Christians all, — re - joice ___ with heart and soul _ and voice! __
2 Good Christians all, — re - joice ___ with heart and soul _ and voice! __
3 Good Christians all, — re - joice ___ with heart and soul _ and voice! __

list - en now to what we say, Je - sus Christ is born to-day;
hear the news of end - less bliss, Je - sus Christ was born for this:
now you need not fear the grave; Je - sus Christ was born to save:

ox and ass be - fore him bow and he is in ___ the man - ger now!
he has o - pened hea - ven's door and we are blessed for ev - er - more!
come at his most gra - cious call to find sal - va - tion, one and all!

Christ is born to - day; ___ Christ is born to - day! __
Christ was born for this; ___ Christ was born for this. __
Christ was born to save; ___ Christ was born to save! __

Music: fourteenth-century German melody (later form)
arranged J Stainer (1840-1901)
based on harmony R L Pearsall (1795-1856)

Words: In dulci jubilo (fourteenth century)
J M Neale (1818-1866)

Come to Bethlehem

2nd verse laing then 3rd verse is 12 with words

Pieds en l'air

1 Come — to Beth - le - hem and see — the new - born king,
2 He, — the Lord of all be - fore — our race — be - gan,

come — and lay your heart be - fore — him while — you sing:
loves — to be and call him - self — the Son — of Man;

he, — the God of earth — and hea - ven, Lord — of all,
ho - ly Ma - ry, vir - gin mo - ther, gave — him birth —

lies — with- in the man - ger of — an ox - 's stall; born — of God, the Fa - ther
see — her meek- ly kneel be - fore him on — the earth. Let — us kneel with her and

in — the bliss — a - bove, born — a ba - by in — a sta - ble for — our love.
lov - ing - ly a - dore Christ — her son, our God — and king — for ev - er - more!

If this is sung in harmony it is suggested that the lower voices sing to *Ah* or hum.

Music: Peter Warlock (1894-1930)
© arranged David Iliff †

Words: A Gregory Murray
© 1956 J Curwen and Sons Limited
Sole selling agents William Elkin Music Services

Rejoice with heart and voice

Gaudete

TENOR

Re - joice with heart and voice! now is our Sav - iour

BASS

_of the vir - gin Ma - ry born — so re - joice!

SOPRANO ALTO

Re - joice with heart and voice! now is our Sav - iour

TENOR BASS

_of the vir - gin Ma - ry born — so re - joice!

Fine

SOPRANO and ALTO

1 At this time our God ful - fils___ all our ex - pec - ta - tion:
2 God of God when time be - gan, Lord of all cre - a - tion:
3 Al - le - lu - ia! Let us sing hymns of ad - or - a - tion.

let us of - fer hearts and wills___ in re - de - di - ca - tion.
we re - vere the Son of Man at his in - car - na - tion.
bles - sing Christ our wor - thy king in this ce - le - bra - tion!

Music: Medieval carol
© arranged John Barnard †

Words: from the Latin
© Michael Perry †

Sing, oh sing, this happy morn

73

England's Lane

1 Sing, oh — sing, this hap-py morn, for to us a — child is born,
2 God of — God, and Light of light, comes with mer - cies — in - fin - ite
3 God with — us, Em - man - u - el, deigns for ev - er — now to dwell —

and to — us a Son is given; God comes down - to — earth from heaven:
join - ing — in a won-drous plan — heaven to earth, — and — God to man:
now on — A-dam's fal-len race sends the ful - ness - of his grace:

Sing, oh — sing, this hap-py morn, — Je - sus Christ to - day is born!

4 God comes down that we may rise,
lifted up into the skies;
Christ is Son of Man, that we,
children of our God may be:
Sing, oh sing, this happy morn,
Jesus Christ today is born!

5 Come, renew us Lord, we pray,
with your Spirit day by day;
that we ever may be one
with the Father and the Son.
Sing, oh sing, this happy morn,
Jesus Christ today is born!

Music: English traditional melody
arrangement G Shaw (1879-1943)
© arrangement Oxford University Press

Words: C Wordsworth (1807-1885)
© in this version Word & Music †

74   Christians, make a joyful sound

Resonet in laudibus (i)

PIANO or ORGAN

mf

1 Christ - ians, make a joy - ful sound, sing to all the
2 Might - y God, Em - man - u - el — prince of whom the
3 Come, you choirs, with glad - ness sing, in - stru -ments of
4 Love is here to seek and save — hea ven's mas - ter

world a - round: he is in a man - ger found,
pro - phets tell, child an -nounced by Ga - bri - el, the
mu - sic bring — ea - ger to pro - claim the king, the
as a slave: God so loved the world he gave

ho - ly One, the in - fant son of Ma - ry.

Let the peo - ple join to say that Christ the Lord is

born to - day, till the ve - ry earth shall raise the

song of praise: 'No - well, no - well —

Christ is born, the in - fant son of Ma - ry!'

Another arrangement of this tune, without refrain, appears at number 52.

Music: fourteenth-century German melody
© arranged John Barnard †

Words: from the Latin (c 1500)
© Michael Perry †

75   God of God, the uncreated

Corde natus

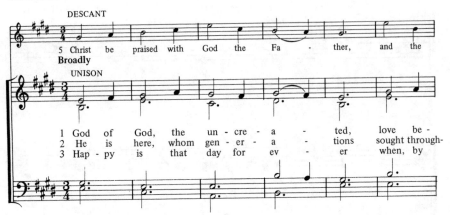

DESCANT

5 Christ be praised with God the Fa - ther, and the

Broadly

UNISON

1 God of God, the un - cre - a - ted, love be -
2 He is here, whom gen - er - a - tions sought through-
3 Hap - py is that day for ev - er when, by

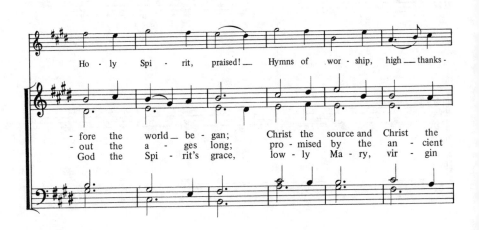

Ho - ly Spi - rit, praised! Hymns of wor - ship, high thanks -

- fore the world be - gan; Christ the source and Christ the
- out the a - ges long; pro - mised by the an - cient
God the Spi - rit's grace, low - ly Ma - ry, vir - gin

- giv - ing e - cho, e - cho through a world a - mazed:

end - ing, Son of God and Son of Man, Lord of
pro - phets — just - ice for a world of wrong, God's sal -
mo - ther, bore the sav - iour of our race. Man and

hon - our, ma - jes - ty, do - min - ion! Songs of vic - to -

all the things that have _____ been, mas - ter of the e -
- va - tion for the faith - ful: him we praise in
child, the world's re - deem - er now dis - plays his

- ry be raised ev - er - more and ev - er - more!

- ter - nal plan, ev - er - more and ev - er - more. _____
end - less song ev - er - more and ev - er - more. _____
sa - cred face ev - er - more and ev - er - more. _____

4 Praise him, heaven of heavens,
  praise him, angels in the height;
  priests and prophets, bow before him,
  saints who longed to see this sight.
  Let no human voice be silent,
  in his glory hearts unite
      evermore and evermore!

5 Christ be praised with God the Father,
  and the Holy Spirit, praised!
  Hymns of worship, high thanksgiving
  echo through a world amazed:
  honour, majesty, dominion!
  Songs of victory be raised
      evermore and evermore!

Words: after Prudentius (348-c 413)
J M Neale (1818-1866) and
Music: *Piae Cantiones* (1582)   H W Baker (1821-1877)
© arranged with descant David Iliff †   © in this version Jubilate Hymns †

76 Ding-dong, ding

Ding-dong ding

Ding - dong, ding, ___ ding - a - dong - a - ding; ding - dong, ding - dong,

ding - a - dong - ding.

Wake then, Christ - ian, come and lis - ten ___
Tell the sto - ry how from glo - ry ___

how the mer - ry church ___ bells ring, and from steep - le
God came down at Christ - mas - tide, bring-ing glad - ness, ___

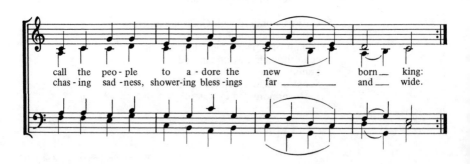

call the peo - ple to a - dore the new - born ___ king:
chas - ing sad - ness, shower-ing bless-ings far ___ and ___ wide.

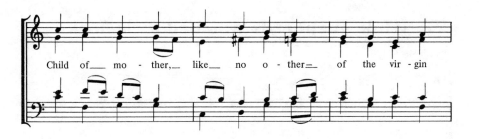

Child of__ mo - ther,__ like__ no o - ther__ of the vir - gin

Ma - ry__ born, to a sta - ble — this no fa - ble —

God came down on Christ - mas morn. Ding-dong, ding,__

ding- a -dong- a - ding; ding- dong, ding - dong, ding - a -dong-ding.

Music: *Piae Cantiones* (1582)
arranged G R Woodward (1848-1934)

Words: from *Piae Cantiones* (1582)
G R Woodward (1848-1934)
© in this version Word & Music †

77 While shepherds watched their flocks

Winchester Old

1 While shep - herds watched their flocks by night, all
2 'Fear not'— said he — for might - y dread had
3 'To you in Da - vid's town this day is

seat - ed on the ground, the an - gel of the
seized their trou - bled mind — 'Glad ti - dings of great
born of Da - vid's line a sav - iour, who is

Lord came down and glo - ry shone a - round.
joy I bring to you and all man - kind:
Christ the Lord. And this shall be the sign:

4 'The heavenly babe you there shall find
to human view displayed,
all tightly wrapped in swathing bands
and in a manger laid.'

5 Thus spoke the seraph, and forthwith⌣
appeared a shining throng⌣
of angels praising God, who thus⌣
addressed their joyful song:

Music: T Este's *Psalmes* (1592)
arranged W H Monk (1823-1889)
© verse 6 arranged with descant John Barnard †

Words: N Tate (1652-1715)

78   Go, tell it on the mountain

Go, tell it on the mountain

Go, tell __ it on the moun - tain, ov - er the hills and

ev - ery - where; __ go, tell __ it on the moun - tain that

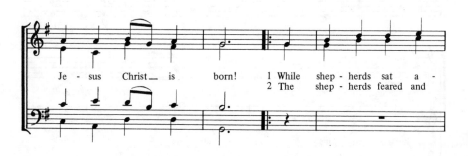

Je - sus Christ __ is born!   1 While shep - herds sat a -
2 The shep - herds feared and

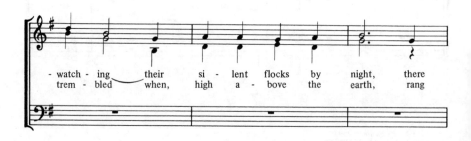

- watch - ing __ their si - lent flocks by night, there
trem - bled when, high a - bove the earth, rang

shone through-out the hea - vens   a   great and   glo - rious
out   the   an - gel   cho - rus   that   hailed our   Sav - iour's
(ATB) Ah _____

light. _____   Go,   tell __ it on the   moun - tain,
birth. _____

o - ver   the hills and   ev - ery - where; __   go,   tell __ it on the

v1   v2

moun - tain that   Je - sus   Christ __ is   born!   born!

Music: traditional melody
© arranged John Barnard †   Words: traditional

79   **From highest heaven**

Echo Carol

1 From high-est heaven where prais-es ring (from high-est heaven where
2 He who in ma - je - sty ar-rayed, (he who in ma - je -
3 Let hu-man power and pomp and pride (let hu - man power and
4 To God the Fa - ther, Spi - rit, Son, (to God the Fa - ther,

prais - es ring) good news I bring (good news I bring),
- sty ar - rayed,) with - out our aid, (with - out our aid)
pomp and pride), both far and wide (both far and wide),
Spi - rit, Son), the Three - in - One (the Three - in - One),

songs to sing (songs to sing): 'Je - sus is born to
all has made (all has made): see him in hum - ble
be de - nied (be de - nied): God is come down at
praise be done (praise be done) for grace and hope this

be your king!' ('Je - sus is born to be your king!')
man - ger laid, (see him in hum - ble man - ger laid).
Christ - mas - tide! (God is come down at Christ - mas - tide!)
day be - gun! (for grace and hope this day be - gun!)

*These chords should be sustained for two beats to create an overlap.

Music: Martin Luther (1483-1546)
© arranged John Barnard †

Words: after M Luther (1483-1546)
© Michael Perry †

Silent night

Stille nacht

1 Silent night! holy night! all is calm,
all is bright round the virgin and her child:
holy infant so tender and mild,
sleep in heavenly peace; sleep in heavenly peace!

2 Silent night! holy night! shepherds quail
at the sight, glory streams from heaven afar:
heavenly hosts sing 'Alleluia,
Christ the saviour is born, Christ the saviour is born!'

3 Silent night! holy night! Son of God,
love's pure light: radiant beams your holy face
with the dawn of saving grace,
Jesus, Lord, at your birth, Jesus, Lord, at your birth.

Music: F X Gruber (1787-1863)
© arranged David Iliff †

Words: after J Möhr (1792-1848)
J F Young (1820-1885)

81 When came in flesh the incarnate Word
(Bellman's Carol)

Bellman's Carol

1 When came in flesh the incarnate Word, the
2 When comes the Saviour at the last, from
3 Then shall the pure in heart be blessed—in

heed-less world slept on, and only watch-ing
east to west shall shine his awe-some light; the
peace he'll come to them as once he lay at

shep-herds heard the news of God's own Son.
earth a-ghast shall trem-ble at the sign.
Ma-ry's breast in dis-tant Beth-le-hem:

4 In peace, to humble love and faith,
   and yet more strong to save;
   more strong by having
      bowed to death,
   by having burst the grave.

5 Lord, who could dare
      see you descend
   in state, unless he knew
   you are the sorrowing sinner's
      friend,
   the gracious and the true?

6 Dwell in our hearts,
      O Saviour blessed:
   so shall your advent's dawn
   become the knowing
      of love's guest,
   the veil of night withdrawn!

Music: English traditional melody
© arranged David Iliff †

Words: J Anstice (1808-1836)
© in this version Word & Music †

When came in flesh the incarnate Word 82
(St Stephen)

St Stephen

1 When came in flesh the in - car - nate___ Word, the ___
2 When comes the Sav - iour ___ at the ___ last, from ___
3 Then shall the pure in ___ heart be ___ blessed— in ___

heed - less ___ world slept ___ on, and on - ly watch - ing ___
east to ___ west shall ___ shine his awe - some light; the ___
peace he'll ___ come to ___ them as once he lay at ___

shep - herds ___ heard the news of ___ God's own ___ Son.
earth ___ a - ghast shall trem - ble ___ at the ___ sign.
Ma - ry's ___ breast in dis - tant ___ Beth - le - hem:

4 In peace, to humble love and faith
and yet more strong to save;
more strong by having
bowed to death,
by having burst the grave.

5 Lord, who could dare,
see you descend⌣
in state, unless he knew⌣
you are the sorrowing sinner's
friend,
the gracious and the true?

6 Dwell in our hearts,
O Saviour blessed:
so shall your advent's dawn
become the knowing
of love's guest,
the veil of night withdrawn!

Music: W Jones (1726-1800)

Words: J Anstice (1808-1836)
© in this version Word & Music †

Infant holy

Infant holy

1 In - fant ho - ly, in - fant low - ly, for his bed a cat - tle stall; —
2 Flocks were sleep-ing, shep-herds keep-ing vi - gil till the morn-ing new, —

ox - en low - ing, lit - tle know - ing Christ the babe is Lord of all.
saw the glo - ry, heard the sto - ry — ti - dings of a gos - pel true.

Swift are wing - ing an-gels sing-ing, no - wells ring-ing, tid - ings bring-ing:
Thus re - joic - ing, free from sor - row, prais - es voic - ing greet to - mor-row:

Christ the babe is Lord of all; — Christ the babe is Lord of all!
Christ the babe was born for you; — Christ the babe was born for you!

Music: Polish traditional melody
arranged A E Rusbridge (1917-1969)
© arrangement Mrs R Rusbridge

Words: from the Polish
E M G Reed (1885-1933)

Hark! the herald angels sing

Mendelssohn

1 Hark! the her - ald an - gels sing __ glo - ry to the new-born King;
2 Christ, by high - est heaven a - dored, __ Christ the ev - er - last-ing Lord:

peace on earth and mer -cy mild, __ God and sin - ners re - con-ciled!
late in time be - hold him come, __ off-spring of a vir - gin's womb;

Joy - ful all you na - tions rise, __ join the tri - umph of the skies; __
veiled in flesh the God-head see, __ hail the in-car - nate De - i - ty! __

with the an-gel - ic host pro -claim, 'Christ is __ born in Beth-le - hem':
pleased as man with man to dwell, Je - sus __ our Em-man- u - el:

Hark! the her - ald an - gels sing glo - ry __ to the new-born King.

born that we no more may die; born to raise us from the earth, born to give us se-cond birth: Hark! the her-ald an-gels sing glo-ry to the new-born King.

Music: F Mendelssohn (1809-1847)
© verse 3 arranged with descant Christopher Robinson

Words: C Wesley (1707-1788) and others

85   Hear the skies around

Rajske strune zadonite

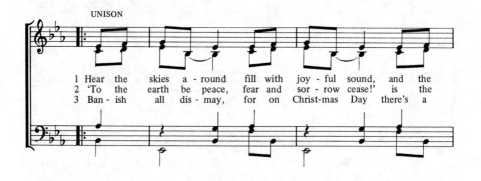

1 Hear the skies a - round fill with joy - ful sound, and the
2 'To the earth be peace, fear and sor - row cease!' is the
3 Ban - ish all dis - may, for on Christ-mas Day there's a

praise of an - gels_____ ring; hear the
birth - day news they_____ bring. 'To the
song of hope to_____ sing; ban - ish

skies a - round fill with joy - ful sound, and the
earth be peace, fear and sor - row cease.' is the
all dis - may, for on Christ - mas Day there's a

praise of an - gels ____ ring: Sing - ing
birth - day news they____ bring: Sing - ing
song of hope to ____ sing: Sing - ing

'Glo - ry in the high - est,' sing - ing 'Glo - ry to the
'Glo - ry in the high - est,' sing - ing 'Glo - ry to the
'Glo - ry in the high - est,' sing - ing 'Glo - ry to the

King!' Hear the skies a - round fill with
King!' 'To the earth be peace, fear and
King!' Ban - ish all dis - may, for on

joy - ful sound, and the praise of an - gels ____ ring.
sor - row cease!' is the birth - day news they____ bring.
Christ - mas Day there's a song of hope to____ sing!

Music: Jugoslavian melody
© arranged David Iliff †

Words: after the Jugoslavian carol
© Michael Perry †

86   Angels from the realms of glory

Iris

1 An - gels from the ___ realms ___ of glo - ry, ___
2 Shep - herds in the ___ fields ___ a - bid - ing,
3 Wise men, leave your ___ con - tem - pla - tions! ___
4 Though an in - fant ___ now ___ we view him, ___

wing your ___ flight through ___ all the earth;
watch - ing ___ by your ___ flocks at night,
bright - er ___ vi - sions ___ shine a - far;
he will ___ share his ___ Fa - ther's throne,

her - alds of cre - a - tion's sto - ry, ___
God with man is ___ now re - sid - ing: ___
seek in him the ___ hope of na - tions,
ga - ther all the ___ na - tions to him; ___

now pro - claim Mes - si - ah's birth!
see, there ___ shines the ___ in - fant light!
you have ___ seen his ___ na - tal star:
ev - ery ___ knee shall ___ then bow down:

DESCANT

Come _____ and wor - ship _

Come _____ and _ wor - ship _

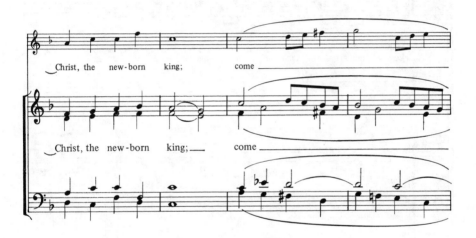

Christ, the new-born king; come _____

Christ, the new-born king; ___ come _____

_____ and wor - ship, wor-ship Christ the new - born _ king!

_____ and _ wor - ship, wor-ship Christ the new - born _ king!

Music: French melody
© arranged with descant John Barnard †

Words: J Montgomery (1771-1854)
© in this version Jubilate Hymns †

87   # Softly, a shepherd is singing
(Choir arrangement)

The Angels and the Shepherds

1 Soft - ly, — a — shep - herd— is — sing - ing — his— song
2 Her - ald - ing— an - gels— are— sing - ing— their. song,
3 Lov - ing - ly— Ma - ry— is — sing - ing— her — song,

o - ver — the— Beth - le - hem— hills — all — night— long:
won - der - ful— words — that — to — hea - ven — be - long:
bear - ing — the— child — who— will— bear — all — our — wrong:

*See note at the end of this arrangement.

Night-time is pass-ing—wait for the dawn-ing! Praise him who brings us joy in the morn-ing:

Al - le - lu - ia!

4 Wor-ship - ping— Je - sus,— we— sing a — new— song — Beth-le - hem's—

baby, our saviour so strong: Night-time is passing—wait for the dawning!

Praise him who brings us joy in the morning: Al - le - lu - ia!

Where possible, the first eight bars of verses 1 and 3 should be sung by a solo boy and girl respectively.

The 3-part harmony is optional and the bottom part may be omitted if 2-part harmony is preferred. The 2-part version is particularly suited to men's voices.

The 4-part harmony arrangement at number 88, if sung a tone higher is entirely compatible with the piano accompaniment offered here; but it is suggested that 4-part harmony should only be used for verses 2 and 4.

Music: Czech melody
© arranged John Barnard †

Words: © Paul Wigmore †

Softly, a shepherd is singing

88

The Angels and the Shepherds

For a more elaborate arrangement of this carol see the previous pages and the note at the bottom of the facing page.

Music: Czech melody
© arranged John Barnard †

Words: © Paul Wigmore †

89 All my heart this night rejoices
(Bonn)

Bonn

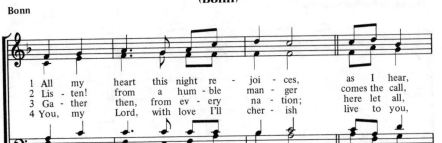

1 All my heart this night re - joi - ces, as I hear,
2 Lis - ten! from a hum - ble man - ger comes the call,
3 Ga - ther then, from ev - ery na - tion; here let all,
4 You, my Lord, with love I'll cher - ish live to you,

far and near, sweet - est an - gel voi - ces. 'Christ is
'One and all, run from sin and dan - ger! Christ - ians
great and small, kneel in a - dor - a - tion; love him
and with you dy - ing, shall not per - ish, but shall

born!' their choirs are sing - ing, till the air
come, let no - thing grieve you: you are freed!
who with love is yearn - ing: Hail the star
dwell with you for ev - er: joy di - vine

ev - ery - where now with joy is ring - ing.
All you need I will sure - ly give you.
that from far bright with hope is burn - ing!
shall be mine that can al - ter nev - er.

Music: J Ebeling (1637-1676)

Words: after P Gerhardt (1607-1676)
C Winkworth (1827-1878)
© in this version Word & Music †

All my heart this night rejoices 90

(All my heart)

All my heart

1 All my heart this night re - joi - ces, as I hear, far and
2 Lis - ten! from a hum-ble man - ger comes the call, 'One and
3 Ga-ther then, from ev - ery na - tion; here let all, great and
4 You, my Lord, with love I'll cher - ish, live to you, and with

near, sweet - est an - gel __ voi - ces. 'Christ is born!' their choirs are
all, run from sin __ and __ dan - ger! Christ-ians come, let no-thing
small, kneel in a - dor - a - tion; love him who with love is
you __ dy - ing, shall __ not __ per - ish, but shall dwell with you for

sing - ing, till the air ev - ery - where now with
grieve you: you are freed! All you need I will
yearn - ing: Hail the star that from far bright with
ev - er: joy di - vine shall be mine that can

vv 1-3   v 4

joy ____ is ring - ing.
sure - ly give you.'
hope ____ is burn - ing!
al - ter   nev - er. ____

Music: © David Peacock †

Words: after P Gerhardt (1607-1676)
C Winkworth (1827-1878)
© in this version Word & Music †

91   From east to west

This endris nyght

1 From east to west, __ from shore __ to shore, let
2 He did not spurn __ the ox - 's stall, nor
3 For us the world's __ Cre - a - tor wears the

earth a - wake __ and sing: __ the ho - ly child that
scorn the man - ger bed; __ there God whose mer - cy
fa - shion of __ a slave; __ our hu - man flesh the

Ma - ry bore is Christ, the Lord and King! __
feeds __ us all, at Ma - ry's breast was fed. __
Mak - er shares; his crea - ture, comes to save. __

4 To shepherds poor, their Lord most high —
   their Shepherd — was revealed,
   while angel choirs sang in the sky
   across the silent field:

5 All glory be to God above,
   and on the earth be peace
   to all who long to taste his love,
   till time itself shall cease!

A more elaborate arrangement of this tune (with other words) appears at number 176.

Music: fifteenth-century English melody
© arranged David Iliff †

Words: after Sedulius (died c 450)
and J Ellerton (1826-1893)
© in this version Word & Music †

Noel

1 It＿came up-on the＿mid-night clear, that glo-rious song＿of old,
2 With＿sor-row brought by＿sin and strife the world has suf-fered long
3 And＿those whose jour-ney＿now is hard, whose hope is burn-ing low,

from＿an-gels bend-ing near the earth to＿touch＿their harps of gold:
and,＿since the an-gels sang, have passed two＿thou-sand＿years of wrong;
who＿tread the rock-y path of life with＿pain-ful＿steps and slow:

'Peace on the earth, good-will to men from heaven's all-gra-cious king!'
for man at war with man hears not＿the love-song which they bring:
O list-en to the news of love which makes the hea-vens ring!

The world in so-lemn＿still-ness lay to＿hear＿the＿an-gels sing.
O hush the noise, you＿men of strife, and＿hear＿the＿an-gels sing!
O rest be-side the＿wea-ry road and＿hear＿the＿an-gels sing!

-told: then earth and heaven re - newed shall see the

-told: then earth and heaven re - newed shall see the

prince of peace, their king; and all the world re -

prince of peace, their king; and all the world re -

- peat the song which now the an - gels sing.

- peat the song which now the an - gels sing.

Music: English traditional melody
arranged A S Sullivan (1842-1900)
© verse 4 arranged with descant Christopher Robinson

Words: E H Sears (1810-1876)
© in this version Jubilate Hymns †

93   O Prince of peace

Rectory Meadow

1 O Prince of peace whose pro - mised
2 O Child who found to lay your
3 O Christ whom shep - herds came to
4 O Sa - viour Christ, as - cen - ded

birth the an - gels sang with
head no place but in a
find, their joy be ours in
Lord, our ri - sen Prince of

'Peace on earth,' peace be to
man - ger bed, come where our
heart and mind; let grief and
life re - stored, our Love who

us and all be - side,
doors stand o - pen wide,
care be laid a - side,
once for sin - ners died,

Music: Erik Routley (1917-1982)
© Oxford University Press

Words: © Timothy Dudley-Smith

94 Holy, joyful dawn of Christmas

O du fröhliche

1 Ho - ly, — joy - ful — dawn of — Christ - mas, —
2 Ho - ly, — joy - ful — dawn of — Christ - mas, —
3 Ho - ly, — joy - ful — dawn of — Christ - mas, —

love to each — un - worth - y heart,
joy to each — un - worth - y heart,
peace to each — un - worth - y heart,

Je - sus — bring - ing new — be - gin - ning, —
Christ — a - bid - ing, sin - ners — guid - ing, —
an - gels — rais - ing hea - ven's — prais - ing, —

love — to — earth — in — ev - ery part.
joy — to — earth — in — ev - ery part.
peace — to — earth — in — ev - ery part.

Music: Sicilian folk melody
© arranged John Barnard †

Words: from the German
© Paul Wigmore †

A great and mighty wonder

95

Es ist ein' Ros'

1 A great and might - y won - der: re - demp - tion draw - ing near! the vir - gin bears the in - fant, the prince of peace is here! Re - peat the hymn a - gain: 'To God on high be glo - ry, and peace on earth! A - men.'

2 The Word be - comes in - car - nate and yet re - mains on high; the shep - herds hear the an - them as glo - ry fills the sky.

3 The an - gels sing the sto - ry: a - wake O dis - tant lands! re - joice, you hills and val - leys; you o - ceans, clap your hands!

- demp - tion draw - ing near!

prince of peace is here!

earth! A - men.'

Music: German melody
arranged M Praetorius (1571-1621)
© verse 4 arranged with descant David Nield

Words: after Germanus (c 634-732)
J M Neale (1818-1866)
© in this version Word & Music †

96

Still, still, still

Still, still, still

PIANO
or
ORGAN

mp

1 Still, — still, — still, the — ba - by — lies a -
2 Love, — love, — love, no — great - er — love than —

- sleep: yet far a - way are her - ald — voi - ces —
his; while 'Christ the — Lord' the an - gels — name him,

hea - ven — sings and earth re - joi - ces! Still, — still, —
we with — fer - vent hearts ac - claim him. Love, — love, —

still, the — ba - by — lies a - sleep.
love, no — great - er — love than — his!

Music: Austrian traditional melody
© arranged John Barnard †

Words: from the German
© Paul Wigmore †

God is in Bethlehem

1 God to A - dam came in E - den,

hea - ven flow - ered at his feet; all cre - a - tion

* See note at the end of this arrangement.

poco rall.

sang to-geth - er, new - born man on earth_ to greet.___

a tempo

Stars beam - ing bright, still of the night, cry of an an - gel,

splen-dour of light shin - ing on Beth - le - hem:_____

God is in Beth - le - hem!_____ 2 Eve to A - dam

came in E - den, na - ture bloss - omed at ___ their side;

bound in love and blessed in un - ion, per - fect man ___ and

poco rall.   a tempo

pur - est   bride. ___
        poco rall.   a tempo
                         Stars beam - ing bright,

still of the night,   cry of an an - gel, splen-dour of light

shin - ing on Beth - le - hem:_____ God is in Beth - le -

- hem!_____ 3 Sin to A - dam came in E - den,

hea - ven sor - rowed in its heart; tears of grief__ its

gar - den drown - ing, thorns of death_in ev - ery part. __

4 God to us has come — a sa - viour, grace — to sin - ners on the earth; shep - herds greet the in - fant Je - sus, God — and man in vir - gin birth.

poco rall.

Stars beam - ing bright, still of the night, cry of an an - gel,
splen-dour of light shin - ing on Beth - le - hem:
God is in Beth - le - hem!
God is in Beth - le - hem!

This carol may be sung by unison voices, omitting the lower part in verses 2 and 3, and the upper part in verse 4.

Music: © John Barnard †

Words: © Paul Wigmore †

98   On Christmas night

Sussex Carol

PIANO or ORGAN

mf

1 On Christ - mas night all Christ - ians sing ___ to
2 Then let us be no long - er sad, ___ for
3 When sin de - parts be - fore ___ his grace, ___ then
4 All out of dark - ness we ___ have light ___ which

hear ___ the news ___ the an - gels bring; on
our ___ Re - deem - er makes ___ us glad; then
life ___ and health ___ come in ___ its place; when
made ___ the an - gels sing ___ this night; all

Christmas night all Christians sing to hear the news the angels bring: news of great joy for all the earth, news of our merciful King's birth.

let us be no longer sad, for our Redeemer makes us glad when from our sin he sets us free that all should gain their liberty.

sin departs before his grace, then life and health come in its place: angels again with joy may sing for all to us see the new-born King.

out of darkness we have light, which made the angels sing this night. Glory to God, good-will and peace be to us now and never cease!

Music: English traditional melody
© collected Oxford University Press
© arranged John Barnard †

Words: traditional
© collected Oxford University Press
and in this version Jubilate Hymns †

99   Ding-dong! Merrily on high

Branle de l'Official

1 Ding - dong! Mer - ri - ly on high   in heaven the bells are
2 E'en so, here be - low, be - low,   let stee - ple bells be
3 Pray you, du - ti - ful - ly prime your ma - tin chime, you

ring - ing.   Ding - dong! Ve - ri - ly the sky   is
swung - en;   and   i - o,   i - o,   i - o,   by
ring - ers;   may you beau - ti - ful - ly rhyme your

riv - en with an - gels sing - ing:
priest and peo - ple sung - en!   Glo -
eve - time song, you sing - ers:

- ri - a, ho - san - na in ex - cel - sis!

Music: sixteenth-century French melody
© arranged C Wood (1866-1926)

Words: G R Woodward (1848-1934)

When God from heaven to earth came down

I saw three ships

1 When God from heaven to earth came down on
Christmas Day, on Christmas Day, the songs rang out in Beth-lehem town on
Christmas Day in the morn - ing.

SOPRANOS 2 For Christ was born to save us all, on
Christmas Day, on Christmas Day, and laid with - in a man - ger stall on
Christmas Day in the morn - ing.

MEN 3 The shep - herds heard the an - gels sing on
Christmas Day, on Christmas Day, to tell them of the sav - iour - king on
Christmas Day in the morn - ing.

ALL 4 Now joy is ours and all is well, on
Christmas Day, on Christmas Day, so sound the or - gan, chime the bell on
Christmas Day in the morn - ing!

Music: English traditional melody
© arranged David Iliff †

Words: © Michael Perry †

101 Come and sing the Christmas story

All through the night

1 Come and sing the Christ-mas sto-ry this___ ho-ly night!
2 Je-sus, Sav-iour, child of Ma-ry this___ ho-ly night,
3 Lord of all! Let us ac-claim him this___ ho-ly night;

Christ is born: the hope of glo-ry dawns___ on our sight.
in a world con-fused and wea-ry you___ are our light.
king of our sal-va-tion name him, throned___ in the height.

Al-le-lu-ia!___ earth is ring-ing with a thou-sand an-gels sing-ing—
God is in___ a___ man-ger ly-ing, man-hood tak-ing,_ self de-ny-ing,
Son of Man—let___ us a-dore him, all the earth is___ wait-ing for___ him;

hear the mes-sage they are bring-ing this___ ho-ly night.
life em-brac-ing, death de-fy-ing this___ ho-ly night.
Son of God—we bow be-fore___ him this___ ho-ly night.

Music: Welsh traditional melody
© arranged John Barnard †

Words: © Michael Perry †

Adeste fideles

1 O come, all ye faith - ful, joy - ful and tri - um - phant; O
2 God from God, Light from light

come ye, O come ye to Beth - le - hem;
lo, he ab - hors not the vir - gin's womb!

come and be - hold him, born the king of an - gels! O
Ve - ry God, be - got - ten, not cre - a - ted.

come, let us a - dore him, O come, let us a - dore him, O

come, let us a - dore him, Christ the Lord!

glo - ry in the ___ high - est!'
now in flesh ap - pear - ing.

in ___ the ___ high - est!' O come, let us a -
now in flesh ap - pear - ing.

Man.

O come, let us a - dore him, ___
- dore him, O come, let us a - dore him, O

Ped.

ff allarg.

___ O come, let us a -dore him, ___ Christ ___ the Lord!
come, let us a - dore him,___ Christ ___ the Lord!

cresc. allarg.

ff

Music: J F Wade (1711-1786)
arranged mainly by W H Monk (1823-1889)
© last two verses arranged with descant Paul Edwards †

Words: after J F Wade (1711-1786)
F Oakeley (1802-1880) and others

103 **O come, all ye faithful**
(Long version)

Adeste fideles

1 O come, all ye faith - ful, joy - ful and tri - um - phant; O
2 God from God, Light from light

come ye, O come ye to Beth - le - hem;
lo, he ab - hors not the vir - gin's womb!

come and be - hold him, born the king of an - gels! O
Ve - ry God, be - got - ten, not cre - a - ted.

come, let us a - dore him, O come, let us a - dore him, O

come, let us a - dore him, Christ the Lord!

3 See how the shepherds
   summoned to his cradle,
   leaving their flocks, draw nigh with lowly fear:
   we too will thither bend our joyful footsteps.
       O come . . .

4 Led by the starlight,
   Magi, Christ adoring,
   offer him incense, gold and myrrh;
   we to the Christ-child bring our hearts' oblations.
       O come . . .

5 Child, for us sinners,
   poor and in the manger,
   we would embrace thee with awe and love:
   who could not love thee, loving us so dearly?
       O come . . .

6 Sing, choirs of angels,
   sing in exultation!
   Sing, all ye citizens of heaven above,
   'Glory to God in the highest!'
       O come . . .

7 Yea, Lord, we greet thee,
   born for our salvation;
   Jesus, to thee be glory given!
   Word of the Father now in flesh appearing.
       O come . . .

OR, ON CHRISTMAS DAY
7 Yea, Lord, we greet thee,
   born this happy morning;
   Jesus, to thee be glory given!
   Word of the Father now in flesh appearing.
       O come . . .

A descant for verses 6 and 7 appears at number 102.

Music: J F Wade (1711-1786)
arranged mainly by W H Monk (1823-1889)

Words: after J F Wade (1711-1786)
F Oakeley (1802-1880) and others

104   O come all you children

Ihr Kinderlein kommet

1 O come all you children to Beth - le - hem town, and see here a ba - by from hea - ven come down; tread soft - ly and en - ter on this sa - cred night a sta - ble with hea - ven - ly glo - ry a - light.

2 O come all you children, come here to the stall and see here a child who is born Lord of all; more fair than the an - gels in glo - ry is he, more love - ly than cher - u - bim ev - er could be.

3 O come all you children, and stand by his bed, and see gen - tle Ma - ry bend low at his head; see Jo - seph, so hum - ble in won - der - ing joy, kneel down at the feet of this most ho - ly boy.

4 O come then, you children, and hark at the throng of an - gels, all crowd - ing the sky with their song; join in with their prais - es and joy - ful - ly sing your loud - est thanks - giv - ing—for Je - sus the king!

For a more elaborate arrangement of this carol see the next page.

Music: J A P Schulz (1747-1800)
© arranged John Barnard †

Words: from the German
© Paul Wigmore †

O come all you children

(Choir arrangement)

Ihr Kinderlein kommet

SOPRANO and ALTO

PIANO

Bright bell-like sound

O come all you chil - dren to Beth - le-hem town, and see here a ba - by from

hea - ven come down; tread soft - ly and en - ter on this sa - cred

all; more fair than the an - gels in glo - ry is he, more

Ah

love - ly than cher - u - bim ev - er could be.

mf

B   p

Ah

mp O come all you child - ren, and stand by his

B

mp sonore

child - ren, and hark at the throng___ of an - gels, all

crowd - ing the sky with their song; join in with their prais - es and

joy - ful - ly sing___ your loud - est thanks-giv - ing— for Je -

- sus the king!

This arrangement may be sung by unison voices, or, where no tenors and basses are available, two-part harmony may be used in verses 2 and 3. The bass part in verse 3 may be sung, an octave higher than printed, by the altos.

For a simpler arrangement of this carol in 4 parts see number 104.

Music: J A P Schulz (1747-1800)
© arranged John Barnard †

Words: from the German
© Paul Wigmore †

106   Come and hear the joyful singing

Nos Galan

1 Come and hear the joy-ful sing-ing,
2 An-gels of his birth are tell-ing, Al-le-lu-ia, glo-ri-a,
3 Choir and peo-ple shout in won-der,

set the bells of hea-ven ring-ing:
prince of peace all powers ex-cel-ling; al-le-lu-ia, glo-ri-a,
let the mer-ry or-gan thun-der;

God the Lord has shown us fa-vour —
death and hell can-not de-feat him: al-le-lu-ia, glo-ri-a,
thank our God for love a-maz-ing,

Christ is born to be our sav-iour.
go to Beth-le-hem and greet him. al-le-lu-ia, glo-ri-a!
Fa-ther, Son and Spi-rit prais-ing.

Music: Welsh traditional melody
© arranged John Barnard †

Words: © Michael Perry †

Lift you heart and raise your voice 107

Marston St Lawrence

1 Lift your heart and raise your voice; faith-ful peo-ple, come, re-joice— grace and power are shown on earth in the sav-iour's ho-ly birth. Glo - ri - a!

2 Mor - tals, hear what an - gels say; shep-herds, quick-ly make your way, find-ing truth in low - ly guise, wis-dom to con-found the wise. Glo - ri - a!

3 Here he lies, the Lord of all; na - ture's king in cat - tle - stall, God of heaven to earth come down— cross for throne and thorn for crown. Glo - ri - a!

4 Lift your hearts and voi - ces high; then shall glo - ry fill the sky, Christ shall come and not be long, earth shall sing the an - gels' song: 'Glo - ri - a!'

OPTIONAL DESCANT

4 Lift your hearts and voi - ces high; then shall glo - ry fill the sky, Christ shall come and not be long, earth shall sing the an - gels' song: 'Glo - ri - a!'

Music: © Paul Edwards †

Words: © Michael Perry †

108   There's a saviour to see

Rise up shepherd and follow

1 There's a Sa - viour to see on ____ Christ - mas morn —
2 If you take good ____ heed to the an - gel's words —

rise up, shep-herd, and fol - low;_ we will show you the place where the
rise up, shep-herd, and fol - low;_ you'll for - get your ____ flocks, you'll for -

Child is born =____ rise up, shep - herd, and fol - low! _
- get your herds =____ rise up, shep - herd, and fol - low! _

Leave your sheep and leave your lambs — rise up, shep-herd and fol - low;_

leave your sheep and   leave your rams ═   rise up, shep-herd, and

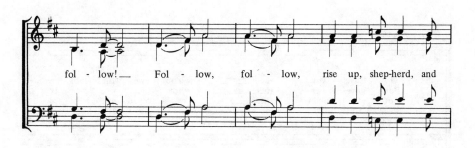

fol - low! ═   Fol - low,   fol - low,   rise up, shep-herd, and

fol - low; ═   hark to the an - gels of Beth-le - hem ═   rise up, shep-herd, and

fol - low, ═   fol - low, ═   fol - low!

109   O leave your sheep

Quittez, pasteurs

1 O leave your sheep, where ewes with lambs are
2 For Love lies there with - in a low - ly
3 You wise men three, ar - rayed in roy - al
4 O Spi - rit blessed, the source of life e -

feed - ing; you shep - herds, hear our mess - age of good
man - ger—the in - fant poor whom an - gel hosts a -
splen - dour, true hom - age pay: your king is born to -
- ter - nal, our souls in - spire with your ce - les - tial

cheer. No long - er weep; the an - gel tid - ings
- dore! Such per - fect care has saved us all from
- day! The star you see its ra - diance must sur -
fire! We make our guest the Christ, the Lord su -

heed - ing, to Beth - lehem haste a - way. Our
dan - ger and brought us to the fold. Now
- ren - der be - fore our Sun most bright. Your
- per - nal, and sing the peace on earth God

Lord, (our Lord,) our Lord, (our Lord,) our Lord is born this
see, (now see,) now see, (now see,) God's faith - ful love re -
gifts, (your gifts,) your gifts, (your gifts,) your gifts are pre - cious
gives, (God gives,) God gives, (God gives,) God gives us by this

hap - py day. Our Lord, (our Lord,) our
- vealed of old. Now see, (now see,) now
in his sight. Your gifts, (your gifts,) your
ho - ly birth; God gives, (God gives,) God

Lord, (our Lord,) our Lord is born this hap - py day.
see, (now see,) God's faith - ful love re - vealed of old.
gifts, (your gifts,) your gifts are pre - cious in his sight.
gives, (God gives,) God gives us by this ho - ly birth.

Music: French traditional melody
© arranged David Iliff †

Words: from the French
John Rutter
© Oxford University Press
and in this version Word & Music †

110   See him lying on a bed of straw

(Calypso Carol)

Calypso Carol

UNISON VOICES

1 See him ly - ing on a
2 Star of sil - ver, sweep a -
3 An - gels, sing_ a - gain the
4 Mine are rich - es, from your

PIANO

mp

bed of straw:_ a draugh - ty sta - ble with an o - pen door;_
- cross the skies,_ show where Je - sus in the man - ger lies;_
song you sang,_ bring God's glo - ry to the heart of man;_
pov - er - ty, _ from your in - no - cence, e - ter - ni - ty;_

Ma - ry cra - dl -ing the babe she bore = the prince of glo - ry is his
shep - herds swift -ly from your stu - por rise_ to see the sav -iour of the
sing that Beth-l'em's lit -tle ba - by can_ be sal - va - tion to the
mine for -give -ness by your death for me,_ child of sor - row for my

name.
world!
soul.
joy.

O now car - ry me to Beth - le - hem__ to

see the Lord__ ap - pear to men!__ just as poor__ as was the

sta - ble then, __ the prince of glo - ry when he

vv 1-3
came.

v 4
came.

For an arrangement which incorporates the melody in the accompaniment see the next page.

111   See him lying on a bed of straw
(Original accompaniment)

Calypso Carol

1 See him ly - ing on a bed of straw: _ a
2 Star of sil - ver, sweep a - cross the skies, _
3 An - gels, sing _ a - gain the song you sang, _
4 Mine are rich - es, from your pov - er - ty, _

draugh-ty sta - ble with an o - pen door; _ Ma - ry cra - dl - ing the
show where Je - sus in the man - ger lies; _ shep-herds, swift-ly from your
bring God's glo - ry to the heart of man; _ sing that Beth-l'em's lit-tle
from your in - no-cence, e - ter - ni - ty; _ mine for - give-ness by your

babe she bore _ the prince of glo - ry is his name.
stu - por rise _ to see the sav - iour of the world!
ba - by can _ be sal - va - tion to the soul.
death for me, _ child of sor - row for my joy.

O now car - ry me to Beth - le - hem___ to

see the Lord___ ap - pear to men!___ just as poor___ as was the

sta - ble then,___ the prince of glo - ry when he came.

For an arrangement with an independent accompaniment see number 110.

112 Little children, wake and listen

Saltash

PIANO
or
ORGAN

_mp_

1 Lit - tle ___ child - ren, ___ wake and lis - ten! songs are ___
2 Shep - herds ___ hur - ry ___ to the sta - ble by the ___

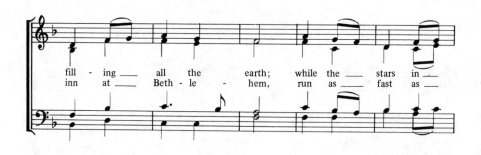

fill - ing ___ all the earth; while the ___ stars in ___
inn at ___ Beth - le - hem, run as ___ fast as ___

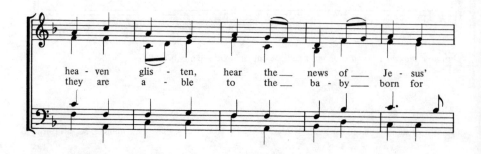

hea - ven glis - ten, hear the ___ news of ___ Je - sus'
they are a - ble to the ___ ba - by ___ born for

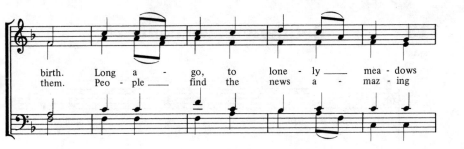

birth. Long a - go, to lone - ly ___ mea - dows
them. Peo - ple ___ find the news a - maz - ing

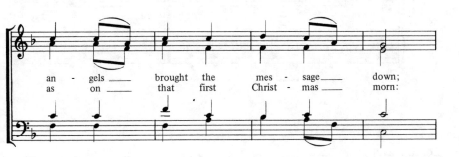

an - gels ___ brought the mes - sage ___ down;
as on ___ that first Christ - mas ___ morn:

still each ___ year through ___ mid - night sha - dows
let us ___ join the ___ shep - herds prais - ing ___

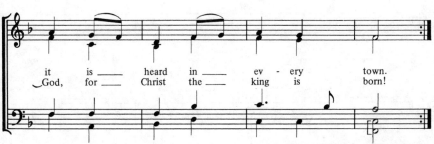

it is ___ heard in ___ ev - ery town.
God, for ___ Christ the ___ king is born!

Music: *Plymouth Collection* USA (1855)
© arranged John Barnard †

Words: verse 1 L H Ward
© 1952 Boston Music Company Incorporated
Reproduced by permission of Chappell Music Ltd
and International Music Publications
verse 2 © Christopher Idle †

113 Bethlehem, we come

Patapan

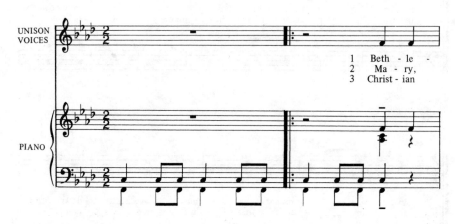

UNISON VOICES

PIANO

1 Beth - le -
2 Ma - ry,
3 Christ - ian

- hem, we come to bring mer - ry dan - ces
may we come to sing mer - ry songs to
peo - ple, now we say mer - ry Christ - mas

for your king!
Christ our king? Step by step and drum by
on this day!

drum, pat - a - pat - a - pan, pat - a - pat - a -

- pan; step by step and drum by drum

step-ping brave - ly, —
step-ping soft - ly, —
step-ping glad - ly, —

Last time

here we come!

114 Christ is born within a stable

Russian Air

DESCANT

3 Peal the bells, and spread the joy - ful news a - broad;

1 Christ is born with -
2 East - ern skies are
3 Peal the bells and

- in a sta - ble:
bright - ly shin - ing,
set them ring - ing,

greet the day when
hope has come up -
spread the joy - ful

hea - ven smiled!
- on the earth;
news a - broad;

Shep - herds, fast as
an - gel songs with
come with faith and

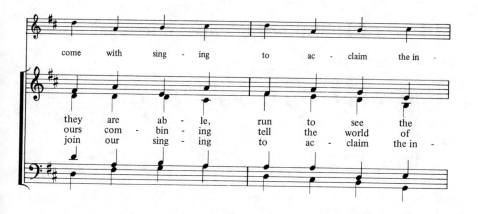

come with sing - ing to ac - claim the in -

they are ab - le, run to see the
ours com - bin - ing tell the world of
join our sing - ing to ac - claim the in -

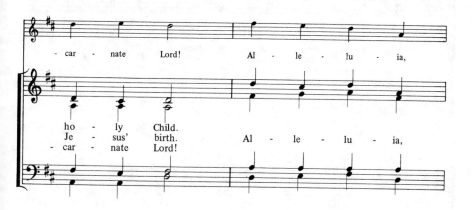

- car - nate Lord! Al - le - lu - ia,

ho - ly Child.
Je - sus' birth. Al - le - lu - ia,
- car - nate Lord!

al - le - lu - ia, al - le - lu - ia! A - men.

al - le - lu - ia, al - le - lu - ia! A - men.

Bells or a glockenspiel may be effectively added to, or used instead of, the sung descant for verse 3.

115   Girls and boys, leave your toys

Zither Carol

1 Girls and boys, leave your toys, make no noise,
2 On that day, far a - way, Je - sus lay —
3 Shep -herds came at the fame of your name,

kneel at his crib and wor - ship him.
an - gels were watch - ing round his head.
an - gels their guide to Beth - le - hem;

For this shrine, Child di - vine, is the sign
Ho - ly Child, mo - ther mild, un - de - filed,
in that place, saw your face filled with grace,

HARMONY

our Sav - iour's here.
we sing your praise.
stood at your door.

Al - le - lu - ia, the

church bells ring, 'Al - le - lu - ia!' the

an - gels sing, al - le - lu - ia from

ev - ery - thing — all must draw near!
ev - ery - thing — our hearts we raise.
ev - ery - thing — love ev - er - more.

Music: Czech folk dance
© arranged John Barnard †

Words: M Sargent (1895-1967)
© Oxford University Press
and in this version Word & Music †

116 Shepherd-boy, tell me

French carol melody

PIANO
or
ORGAN

1 Shep - herd - boy, tell me, why are you sing - ing;
2 Shep - herd - boy, tell me, where are you go - ing;
3 Shep - herd - boy, tell me, why are you kneel - ing;

shep - herd - boy, tell me, what is your song?
shep - herd - boy, tell me, what is your aim?
shep - herd - boy, tell me, what is your prayer?

Glo - ry shone round me, and an - gels came wing - ing;
King in a sta - ble where cat - tle are low - ing:
Christ, be my guard - ing, my sav - ing, my heal - ing;

born is our sav - iour — that is my song.
he is our sav - iour — that is my aim.
love me, O Sav - iour — that is my prayer.

Music: traditional melody
© arranged John Barnard †

Words: from the French
© Paul Wigmore †

A child this day is born

117

Sandys

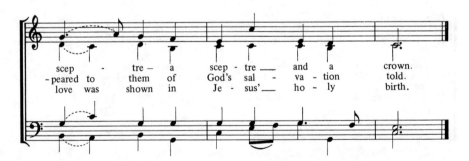

4 They praised the Lord our God,
   our great celestial King:
   now 'Glory in the highest heaven!'
   let all creation sing.

5 And what the angel said,
   did yet in truth appear;
   at Bethlehem they found the child,
   laid in a manger there.

6 Then glory be to God
   who reigns supreme on high;
   with glad thanksgiving, worthy praise,
   and joyful melody!

7 Glad tidings sing to all,
   glad tidings all shall say,
   because the King of all kings
   was born on Christmas Day.

If a shorter version of this carol is needed, verses 3 and 4 may be omitted.

Music: English traditional melody
from W Sandys' *Christmas Carol* (1833)

Words: traditional
© in this version Word & Music †

1, 2, 4

118   Christians, awake

Yorkshire

1 Christ - ians, a - wake, sa - lute the hap - py
2 Then to the watch - ful shep - herds it was
3 To Beth - le - hem these shep - herds swift - ly
4 O may we keep and pon - der in our

morn on which the sav - iour of the
told, who heard the her - ald an - gel's
run to see the won - der of God's
mind God's gra - cious love in sav - ing

world was born; rise to a -
voice: 'Be - hold, I bring good
on - ly Son; they find with
lost man - kind: trace we his

- dore the my - ster - y of love
ti - dings of a ho - ly birth
Jo - seph and the low - ly maid,
foot - steps who re - trieved our loss,

which hosts of an - gels chant - ed from a -
to you and ev - ery na - tion on the ____
the new - born sav - iour in a man - ger ____
from his poor man - ger to his bit - ter ____

- bove! With them the joy - ful
earth: this day has God ful -
laid. In hu - man form their
cross. Saved by his love, un -

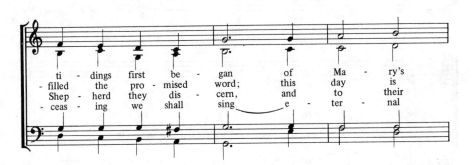

ti - dings first be - gan of Ma - ry's
- filled the pro - mised word; this day is
Shep - herd they dis - cern, and to their
- ceas - ing we shall sing e - ter - nal

in - fant and our God made man.
born a sav - iour, Christ the Lord!
flocks, still prais - ing God, re - turn.
praise to hea - ven's might - y king!

Music: J Wainwright (1723-1768)
arranged W H Monk (1823-1889)

Words: J Byrom (1692-1763)
© in this version Word & Music †

119   See, amid the winter snow

Humility

UNISON

1 See, a - mid the win - ter snow,
2 Low with - in a man - ger lies
3 Say, you hum - ble shep - herds, say

born for us on earth be - low;
he who built the star - ry skies;
what your joy - ful news to - day;

see, the gen - tle Lamb ap - pears,
he who, throned in height sub - lime,
tell us why you left your sheep

pro - mised from e - ter - nal years:
reigns a - bove the cher - u - bim:
on the lone - ly moun - tain steep:

Hail, O ev - er - bless - èd morn! hail, re - demp - tion's

hap - py_ dawn! sing through all Je - ru - sa - lem:_

'Christ is born in Beth - le - hem!'

4 'As we watched at dead of night,
all around us shone a light;
angels singing Peace on earth
told us of a Saviour's birth.'
   Hail, O ever-blessèd morn!
   hail, redemption's happy dawn!
   sing through all Jerusalem:
   'Christ is born in Bethlehem!'

5 Sacred infant, king most dear,
what a tender love was here,
thus to come from highest bliss
down to such a world as this!
   Hail, O ever-blessèd morn!
   hail, redemption's happy dawn!
   sing through all Jerusalem:
   'Christ is born in Bethlehem!'

6 Holy Saviour, born on earth,
teach us by your lowly birth;
grant that we may ever be
taught by such humility.
   Hail, O ever-blessèd morn!
   hail, redemption's happy dawn!
   sing through all Jerusalem:
   'Christ is born in Bethlehem!'

Music: J Goss (1800-1880)

Words: E Caswall (1814-1878)
© in this version Jubilate Hymns †

God rest you merry

God rest you merry

1 God rest you mer - ry, gen - tle - men, let no - thing you dis -
2 At Beth - le - hem in Ju - dah the ho - ly babe was
3 From God our hea - venly Fa - ther a ho - ly an - gel

- may! for Je - sus Christ our sav - iour was
born; they laid him in a man - ger on
came; the shep - herds saw the glo - ry and

born on Christ - mas Day, to save us all from
this most hap - py morn: at which his mo - ther
heard the voice pro - claim that Christ was born in

Sa - tan's power when we were gone a - stray: ___
Ma - ry did nei - ther fear nor scorn: ___
Beth - le - hem and Je - sus is his name: ___

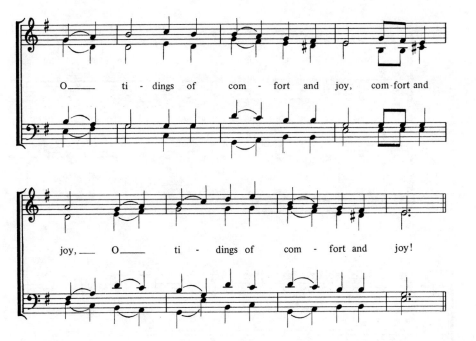

O___ ti - dings of com - fort and joy, com-fort and joy, ___ O___ ti - dings of com - fort and joy!

4 Fear not, then said the angel,
  let nothing cause you fright;
  to you is born a saviour
  in David's town tonight,
  to free all those who trust in him
  from Satan's power and might:
      O tidings of comfort and joy,
      O tidings of comfort and joy!

5 The shepherds at these tidings
  rejoiced in heart and mind,
  and on the darkened hillside
  they left their flocks behind,
  and went to Bethlehem straightway
  this holy child to find:
      O tidings of comfort and joy,
      O tidings of comfort and joy!

6 And when to Bethlehem they came
  where Christ the infant lay;
  they found him in a manger
  where oxen fed on hay,
  and there beside her newborn child
  his mother knelt to pray:
      O tidings of comfort and joy,
      O tidings of comfort and joy!

Music: English traditional melody
arranged J Stainer (1840-1901)
© verse 7 arranged with descant Christopher Robinson

Words: traditional (eighteenth century)
© in this version Jubilate Hymns †

121   The virgin Mary had a baby boy

The Virgin Mary

ba - by___ boy___ and they say that ___ his name is Je - sus.___
ba - by was born___ and they sang that ___ his name is Je - sus.___
ba - by was born___ and they say that ___ his name is Je - sus.___

He come from the glo - ry, he come from the

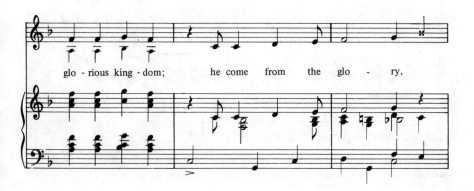

glo - rious king - dom; he come from the glo - ry,

he come from the glo - rious king - dom: O yes, be - liev - er!

O yes, be - liev - er! He come from the

glo - ry, he come from the glo - rious king - dom.

after v3

✗ indicates optional clapping.

Where 2-part harmony is suggested the lower part should be sung by the men
at the printed pitch, not an octave lower.

The addition of claves playing the rhythm ♩. ♩. ♩ will be found effective.

Music: West Indian traditional melody
© collected Boosey & Hawkes
© arranged John Barnard †

Words: West Indian carol
© collected Boosey & Hawkes
source unknown

Christmas for God's holy people

Every star shall sing a carol

PIANO

UNISON

1 Christ-mas for God's ho - ly peo-ple is a time of __ joy and _ peace:
2 Child of Ma - ry, vir - gin mo-ther, pea-sant ba - by, yet our _ king,
3 An - gel ar - mies sang in cho-rus at our Christ's na - tiv - i - ty,

so, all Christ - ian men and wo-men, hymns and ca - rols _ let us raise
cra - dled there a - mong the ox - en: joy - ful ca - rols _ now we sing
he who came to share our na - ture: so we sing with _ gai - e - ty

to our God come to earth, Son of Man, by __ hu - man birth.

4 Shepherds hurried to the manger,
saw the babe in Bethlehem,
glorified the God in heaven:
now we join to sing with them
to our God come to earth,
Son of Man, by human birth.

5 Infant lowly, born in squalor,
prophet, king and great high priest,
Word of God, to man descending:
still we sing, both great and least,
to our God come to earth
Son of Man, by human birth.

Music: Sydney Carter
© Galliard Ltd./ Stainer & Bell Ltd.

Words: © Michael Saward †

Stars of heaven

Cuxham

1 Stars of hea - ven, clear and bright,
2 Sleep - y sounds of beast and byre
3 Wide - eyed shep - herds mute - ly gaze

shine up - on this Christ - mas night. Vast - er far than
min - gle with the an - gel choir. High - est hea - ven
at the child whom an - gels praise. Three - fold gifts the

mid - night skies ___ are its time - less my - ster - ies.
bends in awe ___ where he lies a - mid the straw,
wise men bring ___ to the in - fant priest and king:

Tramp-led earth and sta - ble floor ___ lift the heart to
who from light e - ter - nal came ___ au - re - oled in
to the Lord im - mor - tal, myrrh ___ for an earth - ly

hea - ven's   door =—
can - dle   flame =—   God   has   sent   to   us   his   Son, —
se - pul - chre =—

earth   and   hea - ven   meet   as   one.

4 Heaven of heavens hails his birth,
King of glory, child of earth,
born in flesh to reign on high,
Prince of life to bleed and die.
Throned on Mary's lap he lies,
Lord of all eternities—
   God has sent to us his Son,
   earth and heaven meet as one.

5 'Glory be to God on high,
peace on earth,' the angels cry.
Ancient enmities at rest,
ransomed, reconciled and blessed,
in the peace of Christ we come,
come we joyful, come we home—
   God has sent to us his Son,
   earth and heaven meet as one.

124   Jesus, child of Mary

Hayle

Gently

1 Jesus, child of Mary born, _____
2 To this place of pain and fear _____
3 Infant in a manger laid, _____
4 Angel hosts the skies adorn, _____

Son of God and Lord most high; _____
love descends in human guise; _____
wrapped about with peasant shawl; _____
we with shepherds glorify _____

come to wear a crown of thorn, _____
God in Christ self-emptied here, _____
gift of grace so freely made, _____
Jesus, child of Mary born, _____

bravely come to die.
foolishness most wise.
saviour for us all.
Son of God most high.

Such a night in Bethlehem 125

Jezus malusienki

1 Such a night in___ Beth - le - hem; such a noise and a
2 Such a light on___ Beth - le - hem; such a glare and a
3 Such a sight in___ Beth - le - hem; such a king in a

rush - ing! All the world here, young and old here,
blaz - ing! An - gels wing - ing, hea - ven sing - ing,
man - ger! God a - bove us come to love us

such a crowd and a crush - ing!
shep - herds fear - ful - ly gaz - ing! God is with us,
with the poor and the stran - ger!

God is with us; Christ the Lord is our Sav - iour!

Music: Polish melody
© arranged David Iliff †

Words: © Paul Wigmore †

126   A child is born in Bethlehem

(A child is born)

A child is born

Brightly

UNISON

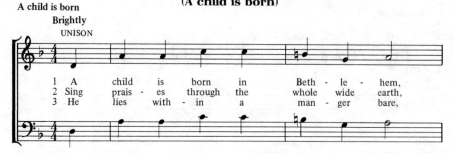

1 A child is born in Beth - le - hem,
2 Sing prais - es through the whole wide earth,
3 He lies with - in a man - ger bare,

Sing — no - well, sing — no - well! the roy - al flower to
Sing — no - well, sing — no - well! for Ma - ry gives the
Sing — no - well, sing — no - well! and shep - herds kneel to

Da - vid's stem, — Al - le - lu - ia, al - le - lu - ia!
Sav - iour birth. — Al - le - lu - ia, al - le - lu - ia!
wor - ship there. — Al - le - lu - ia, al - le - lu - ia!

4 He comes to be our hope of peace,
   Sing nowell, sing nowell!
to bring imprisoned souls release.
   Alleluia, alleluia!

5 Our guilt has found a certain cure,
   Sing nowell, sing nowell!
for Christ makes our salvation sure.
   Alleluia, alleluia!

Music: © Norman Warren †

Words: from the Danish
© Michael Perry †

A child is born in Bethlehem 127

(Sing Nowell)

Sing Nowell

1 A child is born in Beth - le - hem, Sing _ no -
2 Sing prais - es through the whole _ wide _ earth, Sing _ no -
3 He lies with - in a man - ger _ bare, Sing _ no -

- well! the roy - al flower to Da - vid's stem,
- well! for Ma - ry gives the Sav - iour birth.
- well! and shep - herds kneel to wor - ship there.

Al - le - lu - ia, al - le - lu - ia!
Al - le - lu - ia, al - le - lu - ia!
Al - le - lu - ia, al - le - lu - ia!

4 He comes to be our hope of peace,
   Sing nowell!
   to bring imprisoned souls release.
   Alleluia, alleluia!

5 Our guilt has found a certain cure,
   Sing nowell!
   for Christ makes our salvation sure.
   Alleluia, alleluia!

Music: sixteenth-century German melody

Words: from the Danish
© Michael Perry †

128   Shout aloud, girls and boys

Personent hodie

1 Shout a - loud, girls and boys!
4 Boys and girls, voi - ces raise!

Sing to - day and re - joice, lift your heart, raise your voice;
Christ - mas choirs, sweet - ly phrase songs of joy and of praise;

come, and do not wa - ver, God has shown us fa - vour:
leave all care and wor - ry, sing the an - gels' sto - ry:

vir - gin - born, born, born, vir - gin - born, born, born,
Christ is born, born, born! Christ is born, born, born,

R.H.
R.H.

R.H. | L.H.
R.H. | L.H.

8
8

vir - gin - born, Ma - ry's child, Christ is here— our Sav - iour!
Christ is born! Peace on earth — and to God be glo - ry!

R.H.

R.H. | L.H.

8

SOPRANO
ALTO

2 There you lie, Lord of all! For your robe —
3 E - ven now, from a - far wise men seek

TENOR
BASS

pea - sant shawl, for your bed — ox - 's stall;
hea - ven's star, bring - ing gifts where you are:

for your throne a man - ger, home-less as a stran - ger;
gold to bow be - fore you, in-cense to im - plore you,

come to win, win, win, come to win,
myrrh to say, say, say, myrrh to say,

come to win,
myrrh to say,

come to win, win, win, come to win,
myrrh to say, say, say, myrrh to say,

come to win,
myrrh to say,

win, win,
say, say,

come to win,
myrrh to say, come to win hell's do - main —
win, win, myrrh to say 'sac - ri - fice' —
say, say,

come to win,
myrrh to say,

Back to first page for verse 4

spurn - ing death and dan - ger!
there - fore we a - dore you!

Music: *Piae Cantiones* (1582)
verses 1 & 4 arranged G Holst (1874-1934)
© verses 2 & 3 arranged David Iliff †

Words: from the Latin
© Michael Perry †

Ring out the bells

Past three a clock

Ring out the bells — the ___ joy-ful news is break - ing;
ring out the bells ___ for ___ Je - sus Christ ___ is ___ born!

1 An - gels in won - der sing of his glo - ry;
2 Let all cre - a - tion wor - ship be - fore him:
3 Pro - phets have spo - ken — hark to their warn - ing:

shep - herds ___ re - turn - ing tell us the sto - ry.
earth ___ bring ___ him ___ hom - age, hea - ven a - dore him!
sha - dows ___ are ___ pas - sing, soon comes the morn-ing!

Music: English traditional melody
© arranged David Iliff †

Words: © Michael Perry †

PART THREE:
EPIPHANY

130   Jesus Christ the Lord is born

Puer Nobis

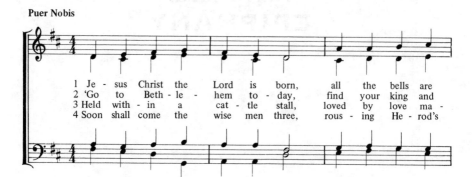

1 Je - sus Christ the Lord is born, all the bells are
2 'Go to Beth - le - hem to - day, find your king and
3 Held with - in a cat - tle stall, loved by love ma -
4 Soon shall come the wise men three, rous - ing He - rod's

ring - ing! ___ an - gels greet the ho - ly One and
sav - iour: ___ glo - ry be to God on high, to
- ter - nal, ___ see the mas - ter of us all, our
an - ger; ___ mo - thers' hearts shall bro - ken be and

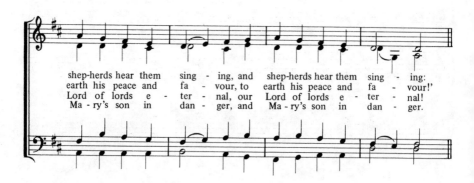

shep-herds hear them sing - ing, and shep-herds hear them sing - ing:
earth his peace and fa - vour, to earth his peace and fa - vour!'
Lord of lords e - ter - nal, our Lord of lords e - ter - nal!
Ma - ry's son in dan - ger, and Ma - ry's son in dan - ger.

5 Death from life and life — from death, our sal - va - tion's
sto - ry: let all liv - ing things give breath to
Christ-mas songs of glo - ry, to Christ-mas songs of glo - ry!

Music: *Piae Cantiones* (1582)
© arranged David Iliff †

Words: after German authors (from the fifteenth century)
© Michael Perry †

131 Where is this stupendous stranger?
(Lismore)

Lismore

1 Where is this stu - pen - dous stran - ger?
2 O most Might - y, O most Ho - ly,
3 O the mag - ni - tude of meek - ness,
4 God all - gra - cious, all - cre - a - tive,

pro - phets, shep - herds, kings, ad - vise:____
far be - yond the se - raph's thought, ____
worth from Worth im - mor - tal sprung;____
whom no wrongs from good dis - suade,

lead me to my Mas - ter's man - ger,
are you then so poor and low - ly
O the strength of in - fant weak - ness,
is in - car - nate — and a na - tive

show me where my Sav - iour lies.____
as un - heed - ed pro - phets taught?____
if the e - ter - nal is so young! ____
of the ve - ry world he made.____

Music: ©Norman Warren †

Words: C Smart (1722-1771)

Where is this stupendous stranger? 132
(Kit Smart)

Kit Smart

UNISON

1 Where is this stu - pen - dous stran - ger?
2 O most Might - y, O most Ho - ly,
3 O the mag - ni - tude of meek - ness,
4 God all - gra - cious, all - cre - a - tive,

pro - phets, shep - herds, kings, ad - vise:
far be - yond the se - raph's thought,
worth from Worth im - mor - tal sprung;
whom no wrongs from good dis - suade,

lead me to my Mas - ter's man - ger,
are you then so poor and low - ly
O the strength of in - fant weak - ness,
is in - car - nate — and a na - tive

show me where my Sav - iour lies.
as un - heed - ed pro - phets taught?
if the e - ter - nal is so young!
of the ve - ry world he made.

Music: Alec Wyton
© 1977 Hope Publishing Company
Carol Stream, Illinois 60188,
All rights reserved, used by permission

Words: Christopher Smart (1722-1771)

133 What Child is this

Greensleeves

1 What Child is this who, laid to rest on
2 Why lies he in so poor a place, where
3 So bring him incense, gold and myrrh, come

Ma - ry's lap, is sleep - ing; whom an - gels greet with
ox and ass are feed - ing? Good Christ - ians, fear for
hum - bly to re - vere him: the King of kings sal -

an - thems sweet, while shep - herds watch are keep - ing?
God is here, and for our peace is plead - ing.
- va - tion brings let faith - ful hearts draw near him.

This, this is Christ the king, whom shep- herds seek and an - gels sing:

haste, haste to bring him praise, the babe, the son of Ma - ry.

Music: English melody before 1642

Words: W C Dix (1837-1898)
© in this version Word & Music †

Stuttgart

DESCANT

5 Je - sus Christ, to you be glo - ry,

1 Beth - le - hem, — what great - er ci - ty
2 Was there ev - er beau - ty bright - er
3 From the East — come men of learn - ing:

Lord of — lords — whom we a - dore: Fa - ther, Son and

can in — fame — with you com - pare? For the gra - cious
than the — star — which shone that night to pro - claim the
rich the — trea - sures that they hold — tri - butes to a

Ho - ly Spi - rit — God be praised for — ev - er - more!

God of hea - ven chose to — meet — his — peo - ple there.
in - car - na - tion of our — God, — the — world's true light?
great - er wis - dom, gifts of — in - cense, — myrrh and gold.

4 Sacrifice, redeemer, saviour:
incense shows that God has come;
gold, our mighty king, proclaims him,
myrrh foretells his silent tomb.

5 Jesus Christ, to you be glory,
Lord of lords whom we adore:
Father, Son and Holy Spirit –
God be praised for evermore!

Music: C F Witt (1660-1716)
© arranged Kenneth D Smith
© descant David Iliff †

Words: after Prudentius (348-c 413)
© Michael Perry †

135 How brightly gleams the morning star

Wie schön leuchtet

1 How bright - ly gleams the morn - ing star! What
2 By you a - lone can we be blessed — then
3 All praise to him who comes to save, who

sud - den rad - iance from a - far de -
deep be on our hearts im - pressed the
con - quered death and spurned the grave! Our

- lights us with its shin - ing?
love that you have borne _____ us;
a - dor - a - tion ris - es.

God's glo - ry breaks up - on the night, and
so make us rea - dy to ful - fil with
to him, the Lamb who once was slain, the

fills our dark - ened souls with light, who long for truth were
fer - vent zeal your ho - ly will, though man - y vex or
Friend whom none shall trust in vain, whose mer - cy yet sur -

pin - ing! Your word, Je - sus,
scorn us. Sav - iour, let us
- pri - ses. Sing, you hea - vens,

tru - ly feeds us, right - ly leads us, life be - stow -
glad - ly hear you, du - ly fear you, long to know
tell the sto - ry of his glo - ry, till his prais -

- ing. Praise such mer - cy ov - er - flow - ing!
you! All we are and have, we owe you.
- es flood with light earth's dark - est pla - ces!

Music: P Nicolai (1556-1608)
arranged F Mendelssohn (1809-1847)

Words: after J A Schlegel (1721-1793)
C Winkworth (1827-1878)
© in this version Word & Music †

136 Three kings from Persian lands

The Three Kings

SOLO: 1 Three kings from Per - sian lands a - far to Jor-dan fol-low the point-ing star; and this the quest of the tra - vel-lers three, where the

TENOR / BASS (*Chorale, pp well sustained): How bright-ly shines the morn - ing star with grace and

* The singers should be placed, if possible, at some distance from the soloist.

new-born king of the Jews may— be; full roy-al gifts they bear for the

truth from heaven a - far! The

truth from heaven a - far! The

pp

king; gold, in - cense,— myrrh— are their of - fer - ing. 2 The star shines

pro - mised tree is grow - ing

pro - mised tree is grow - ing

child— in her— lap they— see; their roy - al gifts they show to the

p

Bride - groom, King di - vine, with

p

Bride - groom, King di - vine, with

p

Bride - groom, King di - vine, with

p

Bride - groom, King di - vine, with

p

king; gold, in -cense, myrrh are their of - fer - ing.___ O child of man,

pp

love be - yond all know - ing. Your word,___

pp

love be - yond_ all know - ing. Your word,

pp

love be - yond all know - ing. Your_ word,___

pp

love be - yond all know - ing. Your word,

pp

Words: after P Cornelius (1824-1874)
and J A Schlegel (1721-1793)
H N Bate (1871-1941)
© Oxford University Press
and in this version Word & Music †

Music: P Cornelius (1824-1874)
arranged I A Atkins (1869-1953)
© Oxford University Press

137   Bright mystical starlight

Infinite Light

The star - light,_ the_ shep - herds,_ the_ an - gels_ and_ kings, all_ tell_ us_ of_ Christ and_ the_ joy_ that he brings.

before verse 2

mp

before verse 3
(Solo)

p

before verse 4

mf

Music: English traditional melody
© arranged John Barnard †

Words: © Paul Wigmore †

138   # The star of heaven

I himmelen, I himmelen

Andante

we   in heaven shall know;   to__ see__ you, Lord God, face to face and__
hea - venly light on earth: how__ pure_ the_ light of   God come down in __

walk where an - gels go! And in that land of ho - ly light no
joy of hu - man birth! And bright-er than the morn-ing sun is

walk where an - gels go! And in that land of ho - ly light no
joy of hu - man birth! And bright - er than the morn-ing sun is

walk where an - gels go! And in that land of ho - ly light no
joy of hu - man birth! And bright-er than the morn-ing sun is

walk where an - gels go! And in that ho - ly light no
joy of hu - man birth! And bright - er than the sun is

guilt of sin, no dread of night, O Lord of earth and heaven!
Je - sus Christ, your ho - ly One, O Lord of earth and heaven!

guilt of sin, no dread of night, O Lord of heaven!
Je - sus Christ, your ho - ly One, O Lord of heaven!

guilt of sin, no dread of night, O Lord of earth and heaven!
Je - sus Christ, your ho - ly One, O Lord of earth and heaven!

guilt of sin, no dread of night, O Lord of earth and heaven!
Je - sus Christ, your ho - ly One, O Lord of earth and heaven!

Music: Swedish melody
arranged J H Åberg
© A B Nordiska Musikförlaget

Words: from the Swedish
© Paul Wigmore †

139   We three kings

Kings of Orient

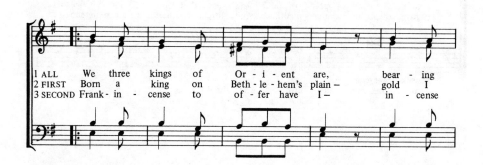

1 ALL   We three kings of Or - i - ent are,   bear - ing
2 FIRST Born a king on Beth - le - hem's plain —   gold I
3 SECOND Frank - in - cense to of - fer have I —   in - cense

gifts we tra - vel a - far —   field and foun - tain,
bring to crown him a - gain: king for ev - er,
tells of De - i - ty nigh: prayer and prais - ing

moor and moun - tain — fol - low - ing yon - der star.
ceas - ing ne - ver, o - ver us all to reign.
all are rais - ing: wor - ship him — God most high!

ALL O ___ star of won - der, star of night, star with roy - al beau - ty bright: west - ward lead - ing, still pro - ceed - ing, guide us to your per - fect light!

THIRD
4 Myrrh is mine — its bitter perfume
   breathes a life of gathering gloom:
   sorrowing, sighing, bleeding, dying,
   sealed in the stone-cold tomb.
ALL O star of wonder, star of night,
   star with royal beauty bright:
   westward leading, still proceeding,
   guide us to your perfect light!

ALL
5 Glorious now behold him arise—
   king and God and sacrifice!
   Heaven sings, 'Alleluia!'—
   'Alleluia!' the earth replies.
   O star of wonder, star of night,
   star with royal beauty bright:
   westward leading, still proceeding,
   guide us to your perfect light!

Music: J H Hopkins (1820-1891)   Words: J H Hopkins (1820-1891)

140   **Brightest and best**

Epiphany Hymn

1 Bright - est and best of the sons of the morn - ing,
2 What shall we give him, in cost - ly de - vo - tion?
3 Vain - ly we of - fer each lav - ish o - bla - tion,
4 Bright - est and best of the sons of the morn - ing,

dawn on our dark - ness and come to our aid;
Shall we bring in - cense and of - ferings di - vine,
vain - ly with gifts would his fa - vour se - cure;
dawn on our dark - ness and come to our aid;

star of the east, the ho - ri - zon a - dorn - ing,
gems of the moun - tain and pearls of the o - cean,
rich - er by far is the heart's a - dor - a - tion,
star of the east, the ho - ri - zon a - dorn - ing,

guide where our in - fant re - deem - er is laid!
myrrh from the fo - rest or gold from the mine?
dear - er to God are the prayers of the poor.
guide where our in - fant re - deem - er is laid!

Music: J Thrupp (1827-1867)

Rejoice and be merry

Gallery Carol

1 Re - joice and be mer - ry in songs and ___ in mirth; O
2 A hea - ven - ly vi - sion ap - peared in ___ the sky; vast
3 And soon in the sky a bright star did ap - pear, which
4 They came and they of - fered myrrh, in - cense ___ and gold — for

praise our re - deem - er, ___ all mor - tals on earth! for
num - bers of an - gels ___ the shep -herds did spy, pro -
led the wise men from ___ the east to draw near; they
God's gra - cious pur - pose ___ these trea - sures fore - told: then

this is the birth - day of Je - sus ___ our king,
- claim - ing the birth - day of Je - sus ___ our king,
found the mes - si - ah, Christ Je - sus ___ our king,
wor - shipped for ev - er be Je - sus ___ our king, who

brought us sal - va - tion — his ___ prais - es we'll sing!

Music: English traditional melody
© arranged David Iliff †

Words: traditional
© in this version Word & Music †

142 **The first nowell**

The first nowell

1 The first now - ell the
2 Then wise men from a
3 At Beth - le - hem they
4 Then let us all with

an - gel did say, was to Beth - le - hem's
coun - try far looked up and
en - tered in, on bend - ed
one ac - cord sing prais - es

shep - herds in fields as they lay; in
saw a guid - ing star; they
knee they wor - shipped him; they
to our hea - venly Lord; for

fields where they lay keep - ing their
tra - velled on by night and
of - fered there in his pre -
Christ has our sal - va - tion

sheep   on   a   cold win - ter's   night ____   that
day   to ____   reach ____   the   place ____   where
- sence   their ____   gold ____   and   myrrh ____   and
wrought   and ____   with ____   his   blood ____   man -

was ____   so   deep:
Je - sus   lay:
frank - in - cense: Now - ell, ____   now -
- kind ____ has   bought:

- ell,   now - ell, ____   now - ell, ____   born is   the

king ____   of   Is - ra - el.

Music: English traditional melody
arranged J Stainer (1840-1901)

Words: unknown (c seventeenth century)
© in this version Word & Music †

143   Mary came with meekness

Noël nouvelet

1 Mary came with meekness, — Jesus — Christ to bear,
2 Angels came with praises, — Jesus — Christ to name,
3 Shepherds came with trembling, — Jesus — Christ to see;
4 Wise men came with treasure, — Jesus — Christ to bless —

laid the Lord of glory in a — manger there.
heaven's choirs exalting him who — bears our shame.
king who, at their bidding, would their — shepherd be.
he who shares all blessings heaven and — earth possess.

We — come rejoicing, Jesus Christ to love:

baby in a manger — king of — heaven above!
baby in a — manger —
baby in a manger —

Music: French traditional melody
© arranged Tom Cunningham †

Words: © Paul Wigmore †

Hark! do you hear

144

The coming of our king

1 Hark! do you hear how the an - gel voi - ces sing,
2 Hush! for the ba - by lies sleep-ing in the hay,
3 See! now a star shin-ing in the east - ern skies,
4 Come! with the wise men your faith-ful hom-age pay,

bear - ing the news of the com-ing of our King?
cra - dled at Beth - le-hem ve - ry far a - way.
guid - ing the wise men to where the in - fant lies.
sing and re - joice that our Lord is born to - day.

Hark! do you hear how the an - gel voi - ces sing,
Hush! for the ba - by lies sleep-ing in the hay,
See! now a star shin-ing in the east-ern skies,
Come! with the wise men your faith - ful hom-age pay,

bear - ing the news of the com - ing of our King?
cra - dled at Beth - le - hem ve - ry far a - way.
guid - ing the wise men to where the in - fant lies.
sing and re - joice that our

Lord is

born to - day!

This may be more effectively performed using ladies' and boys' voices only for the unison sections of verse 2 and men's voices only for the unison sections of verse 3.

Music: Polish melody
© arranged David Iliff †

Words: from the Polish
John Rutter
© Oxford University Press

145 Jesus, you are welcome

Nu zijt wellekome

1 Je - sus, you are wel - come = Je - sus, our dear Lord; from home in far - thest hea - ven you come, a - dored. Life on earth so

2 Shep - herds on the hill - side hear the an - gels' song; from it tells them of a Sav - iour a - wait - ed long: 'Go a - long the

3 Wise men in the dawn - light come with east - ern gold, sweet - est myrrh and in - cense for Christ to hold. Bowed be - fore the

brief be - gin - ning, Christ, e - ter - nal
streets to find him, down a - mong the
ho - ly child they see him long - fore -

Word! From the bells of
throng, ba - by born of
- told, Je - sus Christ who

hea - ven what wel - com - ing is
Ma - ry to save us from all
makes us all wel - come in his

poured!
wrong.' Have mer - cy, Lord.
fold.

Music: fifteenth-century Dutch melody
© arranged John Barnard †

Words: from the Dutch
© Paul Wigmore †

146   As with gladness

Dix

1 As with _ glad - ness   men   of   old   did the guid - ing
2 As with _ joy - ful   steps   they   sped   to that low - ly
3 As they _ of - fered   gifts   most   rare   at your cra - dle
4 Ho - ly _ Je - sus,   ev - ery   day   keep us   in the

star be - hold,   as   with _ joy   they   hailed its _ light, _
man - ger   bed,   there   to _ bend   the   knee be - fore _
plain   and   bare,   so   may _ we   with   ho - ly _ joy _
nar - row   way,   and   when _ earth - ly   things   are _ past, _

lead - ing   on - ward,   beam - ing _ bright: _   so,   most _ gra - cious
Christ whom heaven and   earth   a - dore: _   so   with _ ev - er -
pure   and   free from   sin's   al - loy, _   all   our _ cost - liest
bring   our   ran - somed   souls   at _ last, _   where they _ need no

Lord,   may   we _ ev - er - more   your   splen - dour   see.
- quick - ening   pace _ may   we   seek   your   throne   of   grace.
trea - sures   bring,   Christ,   to   you,   our   hea - venly   king.
star   to   guide,   where   no   clouds   your   glo - ry   hide.

5 In the heavenly country bright none shall need created light —
Christ, its light, its joy, its crown, Christ its sun which goes not down;
there for ev - er may we sing al - le - lu - ias to our king.

Music: C Kocher (1786-1872)
arranged W H Monk (1823-1889) and S Nicholson (1875-1947)
© Royal School of Church Music
© verse 5 arranged with descant John Barnard †

Words: W C Dix (1837-1898)
© in this version Jubilate Hymns †

147 Shepherds came, their praises bringing

Quem pastores laudavere

1 Shep - herds came, their prais - es bring - ing,
  who ___ had heard ___ the an - gels sing - ing:
  'Far from you be fear ___ un - ru - ly,
  Christ is king ___ of glo - ry born.'

2 Wise men whom a star ___ had guid - ed
  in - cense, gold, ___ and myrrh pro - vi - ded,
  made their sac - ri - fi - ces tru - ly
  to the king ___ of glo - ry born.

3 Je - sus born the king ___ of hea - ven,
  Christ ___ to us ___ through Ma - ry gi - ven,
  to your praise and ho - nour du - ly
  be re - sound - ing glo - ry done!

Music: fourteenth-century German melody
arranged R Vaughan Williams (1872-1958)
© arrangement Oxford University Press

Words: from *Quem pastores laudavere* (fifteenth century)
G B Caird (1917-1984)
as revised by the author
© Mrs V Caird

Small wonder the star

No small wonder

1 Small won - der the star, small won - der the
2 Small won - der the kings, small won - der they
3 Small won - der the love, small won - der the

light, the an - gels in cho - rus, the
bore the gold and the in - cense, the
grace, the pow - er, the glo - ry, the

shep - herds in fright; but sta - ble and
myrrh, to a - dore; but God gives his
light of his face; but all to re -

man - ger for God no small won - der!
life on a cross no small won - der!
- deem my poor heart no small won - der!

A more elaborate arrangement for choir and organ appears on the next page.

149

Small wonder the star
(Choir arrangement)

No small wonder

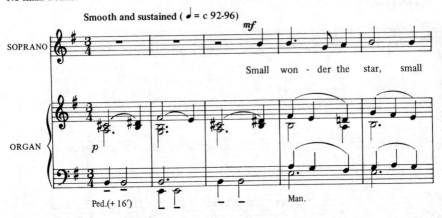

Smooth and sustained (♩ = c 92-96)

SOPRANO

Small won - der the star, small

ORGAN

Ped.(+ 16')   Man.

won - der the light,   the   an - gels in   cho - rus, the

Ped.

shep - herds in   fright;   but   sta - ble and   man - ger for

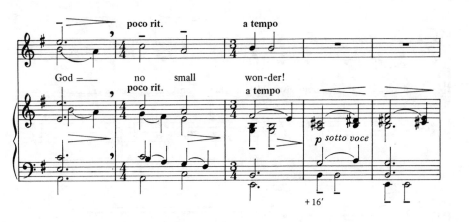

God — no small won-der!

Small won - der the kings, — small won - der they

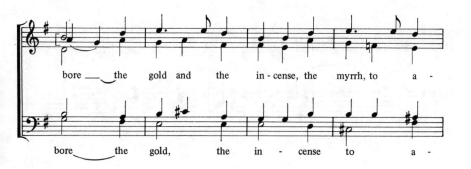

bore — the gold and the in - cense, the myrrh, to a -

bore — the gold, the in - cense to a -

powⵏ-ⵏer, the gloⵏ-ⵏry, the light of his face;— but all to reⵏ-ⵏdeem my poor heart — no — small — wonⵏ-ⵏder!

gloⵏ - ⵏry, the light of his face; but

150   O worship the Lord

Was lebet

1 O wor - ship the Lord in the beau - ty of ho - li - ness,
bow down be - fore him, his glo - ry pro - claim; with
gold of o - bed - ience and in - cense of low - li - ness,
kneel and a - dore him — the Lord is his name.

2 Low at his feet lay your bur - den of care - ful - ness,
high on his heart he will bear it for you,
com - fort your sor - rows and an - swer your prayer - ful - ness,
guid - ing your steps in the way that is true.

3 Fear not to en - ter his courts in the slen - der - ness
of the poor wealth you would count as your own:
truth in its beau - ty and love in its ten - der - ness —
these are the of - ferings to bring to his throne.

4 These, though we bring them in trem - bling and fear - ful - ness,
he will ac - cept for the name that is dear;
morn - ings of joy give for eve - nings of tear - ful - ness,
trust for our trem - bling and hope for our fear.

Verse 1 may be repeated at the end.

Music: melody from MS by J H Rheinhardt, Üttingen (1754)   Words: J S B Monsell (1811-1875)

Jesus, child of gentle Mary 151

The Shepherds' Farewell

1 Je - sus, child of ____ gen - tle Ma - ry, as
2 When ____ you walk a - mong ____ the hea - then and
3 Though __ the clouds of ____ ev - il ho - ver, though

now you leave your low - ly bed
suf - fer tor - ment, grief ____ and pain,
winds of cold in - just - ice blow,

hear the shep - herds' prayer ____ of bless - ing, for ____
shep - herds in their joy ____ im - plore you, re -
an - gels of the Lord ____ sur - round you, pro -

poco f

dan - ger stalks __ the path __ you tread: .
- turn _____ to Beth - le - hem a - gain!
- tect _____ you, guide __ you here __ be - low;

poco f

p

Ma - ry hold you, Jo - seph lead _____ you,
Let the poor, the weak __ and hum - ble
ho - ly child of hu - man mo - ther,

p

God be e - ver at _____ your head;
in your heart of love __ re - main;
God be with you as _____ you go;

f   *mf*   *dim.*

Ma - ry hold __ you, Jo - seph lead you,
let __ the poor, __ the weak __ and hum - ble
ho - ly child __ of hu - man mo - ther,

f   *mf*   *dim.*

God — be ev - ver at — your head! —
in — your heart — of love — re - main, —
God — be with — you as — you go!

poco rit.

Tempo I

vv 1 & 2

God be e - ver at — your head!
in your heart — of love — re main.
God be with — you as — you

v 3

go!

pp

Music: from *L'Enfance du Christ*, Hector Berlioz (1803-1869)
© in this arrangement Jubilate Hymns †

Words: after Hector Berlioz (1803-1869)
© Paul Wigmore †

152　Hush, do not cry

Coventry Carol

* Hush, do not cry, my lit - tle ti - ny child:

child: Lul - la - by, lul - la - lay!

1　O bro - thers, tell what ill be -
2　O sis - ters too, what may we
3　He - rod the king, in his rag -
4　Then woe is me, poor child, to

* The refrain may be omitted, or sung at the start only.

- fell   Beth - le - hem's   town   this ___   day;   let
do   and   save   from   death   to - day   this
- ing,   gave   his   com - mand   this ___   day: his
- see   this   sad   and   sor - ry ___   day;   from

grief   re - cite   these   in - fant's ___
poor   young   thing   to   whom   we ___
men   of   might   in   his   own ___
your   part - ing   we   say   nor ___

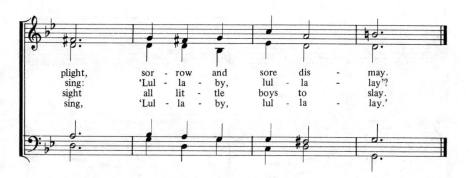

plight,   sor - row   and   sore   dis - may.
sing: 'Lul - la - by,   lul - la - lay'?
sight   all   lit - tle   boys   to   slay.
sing,   'Lul - la - by,   lul - la - lay.'

Music: English melody
© arranged David Iliff † from the version of 1591

Words: R Croo (1534)
© in this version Word & Music †

153   Child, when Herod wakes

Christmas Now

1 Child, when Her - od wakes and hate or ex - ploi - ta - tion
2 Child, when Cae - sar's laws choke love or stran - gle free - dom,
3 Child, when Cai - a - phas sends truth to cru - ci - fix - ion
4 Child, your help - less love brings death and re - sur - rec - tion:

swing their drip - ping swords, from your cross and cra - dle
call - ing dark - ness light, from your cross and cra - dle
to pro - tect his prayers, from your cross and cra - dle
joy - ful - ly we come to your cross and cra - dle

sing a new song.
sing a new song.
sing a new song.
with a new song — Al - le - lu - ia! Al - le - lu - ia!

Music: Peter Cutts
© Oxford University Press

Words: Brian Wren
© Oxford University Press

Faithful vigil ended

Faithful vigil

1 Faith - ful vi - gil end - ed,_____
2 All the Spi - rit pro - mised, _____
3 This your great de - liv - erance ____
4 Christ, your peo - ple's glo - ry! ____

watch - ing, wait - ing cease; ____ Mas - ter, grant your
all the Fa - ther willed, ___ now these eyes be -
sets your peo - ple free; ____ Christ their light up -
watch - ing, doubt - ing cease; ____ grant to us your

ser - vant ____ his dis - charge in peace. ____
- hold ___ it ____ per - fect - ly ful - filled. ___
- lift - ed ___ all the na - tions see. ____
ser - vants ___ our dis - charge in peace. ____

Music: © David Wilson †
© arranged John Barnard †

Words: from Luke 2
The Song of Simeon/Nunc Dimittis
© Timothy Dudley-Smith

155 The Lord of life and glory

Zu Bethlehem geboren

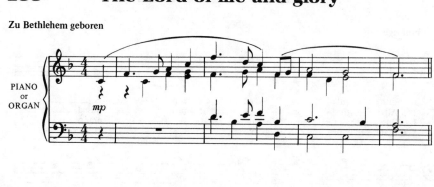

1 The Lord of life and glory came down on earth to
2 But Beth-le-hem of Ju-dah de-spised a king so
3 A vir-gin bore a ba-by, in flesh God man-i-

dwell, and an-gels hailed his com-ing, our
poor; no inn, no house was o-pen to
-fest; the might-y God, the prince of peace found

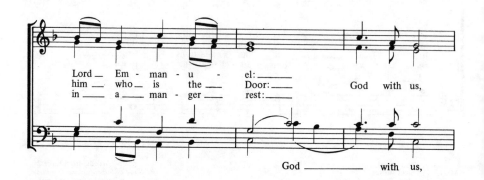

Lord Em-man-u-el:
him who is the Door: God with us,
in a man-ger rest:

God with us,

God with us, our ___ Lord Em - man - u - el!

4 The wise men and the shepherds
  to Jesus made their way;
  to bring their gifts of honour
  and in their worship say:
    'God with us, God with us,
    our Lord Emmanuel!'

5 Since Simeon in the temple
  held Christ in loving hands,
  and Anna saw the saviour,
  his praise has reached all lands:
    God with us, God with us,
    our Lord Emmanuel!

6 So let us praise our saviour,
  lift up our hearts and sing
  of Christ who came to save us
  and lives to be our king:
    God with us, God with us,
    our Lord Emmanuel!

Music: German traditional melody
© arranged John Barnard †

Words: © Kenneth G Hockridge

156   Lord, now let your servant
(North Coates)

North Coates

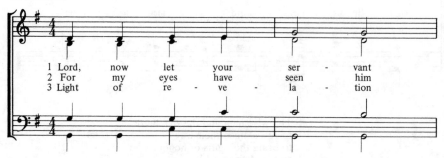

1 Lord, now let your ser - vant
2 For my eyes have seen him
3 Light of re - ve - la - tion

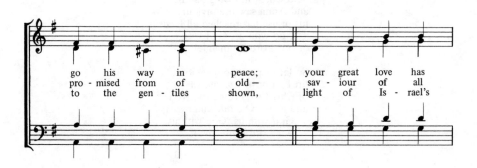

go his way in peace; your great love has
pro - mised from of old — sav - iour of all
to the gen - tiles shown, light of Is - rael's

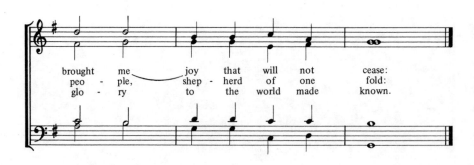

brought me joy that will not cease:
peo - ple, shep - herd of one fold:
glo - ry to the world made known.

Words: from Luke 2
The Song of Simeon/Nunc Dimittis
J E Seddon (1915-1983)
© Mrs M Seddon †

Music: T R Matthews (1826-1910)

Lord, now let your servant

157

(Caswall)

Caswall

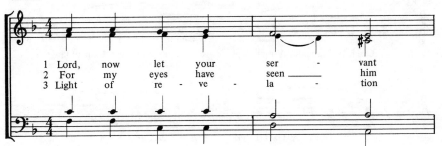

```
1 Lord,    now    let    your    ser -   vant
2 For      my     eyes   have    seen    him
3 Light    of     re - ve - la -          tion
```

```
go      his    way    in    peace;      your   great   love   has
pro - mised   from   of    old —        sav - iour    of     all
to      the    gen - tiles shown,        light  of      Is - rael's
```

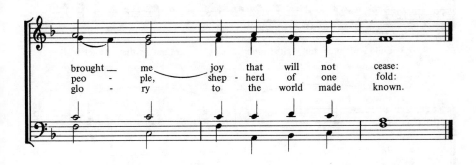

```
brought — me —          joy    that   will   not   cease:
peo -    ple,    shep - herd    of     one   fold:
glo -    ry      to      the    world  made  known.
```

Music: F Filitz (1804-1876)

Words: from Luke 2
The Song of Simeon/Nunc Dimittis
J E Seddon (1915-1983)
© Mrs M Seddon †

158 Child of mine

Child of mine

SOPRANO

1 Child of mine, the Vir-gin sings, child of mine, yet King of kings; pro - mised us by Ga-bri - el, Je - sus Christ, Em-man - u - el.

SOPRANO
ALTO

2 Child of mine—how can this be? Child of mine— what my-ste-ry! But things are as God has planned, all are safe with-in his hand.
But things are as planned; all are safe with-in his hand.

Ah _____ Ah _____

TENOR and BASS

3 Child of mine and gift from heaven; child of mine that God has given.

Ah _____ Ah _____

First born son, and precious boy, born to sor - row, born to joy.

TENOR

4 Child _ of mine, soon_sor-row's dart, child of mine, _ shall _ pierce my heart;

BASS

but _ great joy is ris-ing there, joy _ for all the world to share.

SOPRANO

ALTO

but great joy is there,_ joy for all _ world to share.

S
A

mf   *cresc.*

5 Child _ of mine—a - mong us now, Je - sus Christ, come show us how

T
B

mf   *cresc.*

5 Child of mine—a - mong us now, Je - sus Christ, come show us how —

Love _ has come to drive out fear: all _ are blessed, for God is here!

rall.

Love, _ drive _ out _ fear:_ all are blessed,_ for God is here!

159 The holly and the ivy

The holly and the ivy

1 The hol-ly and the i-vy when they are both full
2 The hol-ly bears a blos-som as white as an-y
3 The hol-ly bears a ber-ry as red as an-y

grown— of —— all the trees that are in the wood, the ——
flower; and —— Ma-ry bore sweet —— Je-sus Christ to ——
blood; and —— Ma-ry bore sweet —— Je-sus Christ to ——

hol-ly bears the crown.
be our true sav - iour. Oh, the ris-ing of the sun —— and the
die for all our good.

run-ning of —— the —— deer, —— the — play-ing of —— the ——

mer - ry or - gan, sweet sing - ing in ___ the ___ choir!

4 The holly bears a prickle
   as sharp as any thorn;
   and Mary bore sweet Jesus Christ
   to wear a cruel crown.
      Oh, the rising of the sun
      and the running of the deer,
      the playing of the merry organ,
      sweet singing in the choir!

5 The holly bears a bark
   as bitter as any gall;
   and Mary bore sweet Jesus Christ
   to suffer for us all.
      Oh, the rising of the sun
      and the running of the deer,
      the playing of the merry organ,
      sweet singing in the choir!

6 The holly and the ivy
   when they are both full grown —
   of all the trees that are in the wood,
   the holly bears the crown.
      Oh, the rising of the sun
      and the running of the deer,
      the playing of the merry organ,
      sweet singing in the choir!

Music: English traditional melody
© arranged John Barnard †

Words: traditional
© in this version Word & Music †

160   On Jordan's bank

Winchester New

1 On   Jor - dan's   bank   the____   Bap - tist's   cry   an -
2 Let   ev - ery   heart   be____   cleansed   from   sin,   make
3 For   you   are   our   sal -   va - tion,   Lord,   our
4 To   heal   the   sick,   stretch _   out   your   hand,   and

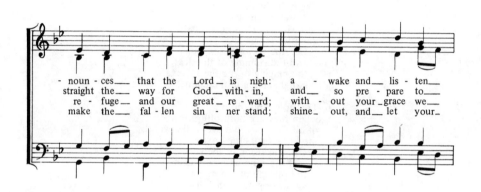

- noun - ces____   that   the   Lord _ is   nigh: a - wake and____ lis - ten____
straight   the____   way   for   God _ with - in,   and____ so   pre - pare   to____
re - fuge____   and   our   great _ re - ward;   with - out   your _ grace   we____
make   the____   fal - len   sin - ner stand;   shine _ out,   and __ let   your____

for ____ he ____ brings glad   ti - dings   of   the   King   of   kings.
be ____ the ____ home where   such   a   might - y   guest   may   come.
waste ____ a - way   like   flowers that   wi - ther   and   de - cay.
light ____ re - store earth's   own   true   love - li - ness once more!

5 To you,— O Christ, all prais - es be, whose

ad - vent sets your peo - ple free; whom with the Fa - ther

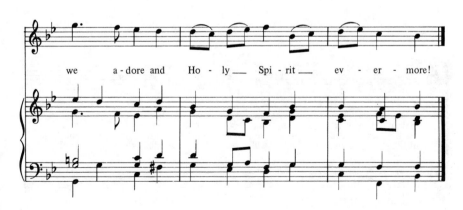

we a - dore and Ho - ly Spi - rit ev - er - more!

Music: *Musikalisches Handbuch* (1690)
© verse 5 arranged with descant John Barnard †

Words: after C Coffin (1676-1749)
J Chandler (1806-1876)
© in this version Word & Music †

161 Songs of thankfulness and praise
(St Edmund)

St Edmund

1 Songs of thank - ful - ness and praise,
2 God re - vealed at Jor - dan's stream,
3 God re - vealed in val - iant fight,
4 Stars shall fall and hea - vens fade,

Je - sus, Lord, to___ you we raise; once re - vealed, when
pro - phet, priest and___ king su - preme; once re - vealed in
con - quer - ing the___ de - vil's might; sins for - giv - en,
sun and moon shall___ dark be made; Christ will then like

hea - ven's star brought the wise men from a - far;
power di - vine chang - ing wa - ter in - to wine;
sick - ness healed, man re - stored and God re - vealed:
light - ning shine, all will see the glo - rious sign;

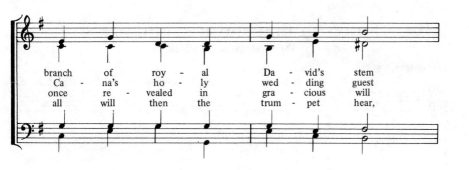

branch of roy - al Da - vid's stem
Ca - na's ho - ly wed - ding guest
once re - vealed in gra - cious will
all will then the trum - pet hear,

in your birth at Beth - le - hem,
keep - ing to the last the best;
ev - er bring - ing good from ill,
all will see the Son ap - pear, Word be - fore the

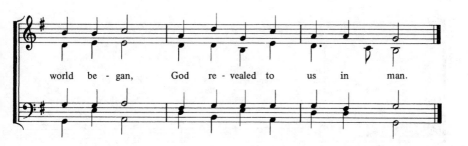

world be - gan, God re - vealed to us in man.

Music: C Steggall (1826-1905)

Words: C Wordsworth (1807-1885)
© in this version Jubilate Hymns †

162   Songs of thankfulness and praise

(St George's, Windsor)

St George's, Windsor

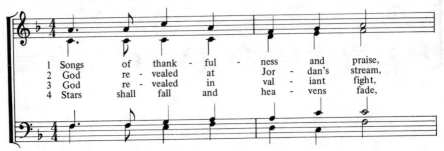

1 Songs of thank - ful - ness and praise,
2 God re - vealed at Jor - dan's stream,
3 God re - vealed in val - iant fight,
4 Stars shall fall and hea - vens fade,

Je - sus, Lord, to you we raise; once re - vealed, when
pro - phet, priest and king su - preme; once re - vealed in
con - quer - ing the de - vil's might; sins for - giv - en,
sun and moon shall dark be made; Christ will then like

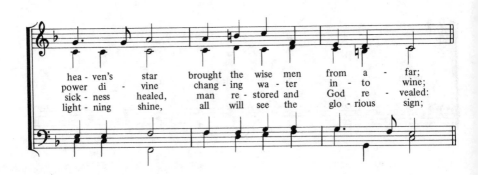

hea - ven's star brought the wise men from a - far;
power di - vine chang - ing wa - ter in - to wine;
sick - ness healed, man re - stored and God re - vealed:
light - ning shine, all will see the glo - rious sign;

branch of roy - al Da - vid's stem
Ca - na's ho - ly wed - ding guest
once re - vealed in gra - cious will
all will then the trum - pet hear,

in your birth at Beth - le - hem,
keep - ing to the last the best; Word be - fore the
ev - er bring - ing good from ill,
all will see the Son ap - pear,

world be - gan, God re - vealed to us in man.

Music: G J Elvey (1816-1893)

Words: C Wordsworth (1807-1885)
© in this version Jubilate Hymns †

PART FOUR:
INCARNATION

163 Word of the Father everlasting

Bergers

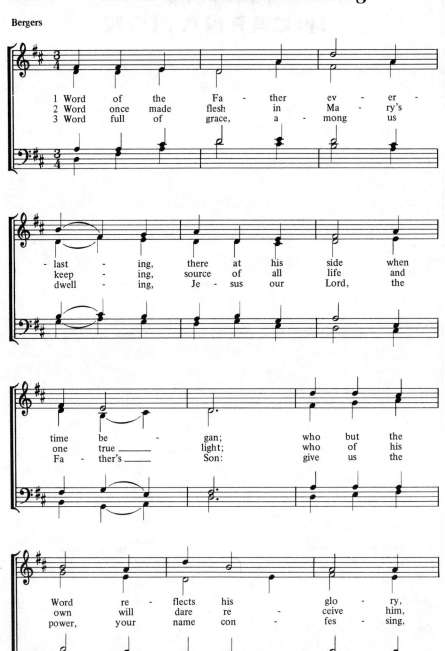

1 Word of the Fa - ther ev - er -
2 Word once made flesh in Ma - ry's
3 Word full of grace, a - mong us

- last - ing, there at his side when
keep - ing, source of all life and
dwell - ing, Je - sus our Lord, the

time be - gan; who but the
one true light; who of his
Fa - ther's Son: give us the

Word re - flects his glo - ry,
own will dare re - ceive him,
power, your name con - fes - sing,

who but the Word may speak to
or to their homes and hearts in -
tru - ly God's chil - dren to be -

man? Word of the Fa - ther
- vite? Word once made flesh in
- come. Word full of grace, a -

ev - er - last - ing, there at his
Ma - ry's keep - ing, source of all
- mong us dwel - ling, Je - sus our

side when time be - gan.
life and one true light.
Lord, the Fa - ther's Son.

Music: French traditional melody
arranged M Shaw (1875-1958)
© Oxford University Press

Words: © David Mowbray †

164   Love came down at Christmas

(Gartan)

Gartan

1 Love came down at Christ - mas,
2 Wor - ship we the God - head,
3 Love shall be our to - ken,

love all love - ly, ___ love di - vine; ___
love in - car - nate, __ love di - vine; ___
love be yours __ and __ love be mine; ___

love was born at Christ - mas =___
wor - ship we our Je - sus =___
love to God and neigh - bour, ___

star and an - gels ___ gave the sign.
what shall be ___ our ___ sa - cred sign?
love for prayer ___ and ___ gift and sign.

Music: Irish traditional melody
© arranged David Iliff †

Words: C Rossetti (1830-1894)
© in this version Jubilate Hymns †

Love came down at Christmas   **165**

(Hermitage)

Hermitage

UNISON

1 Love came down at Christ - mas,
2 Wor - ship we the God - head,
3 Love shall be our to - ken,

love all love - ly, love di - vine;
love in - car - nate, love di - vine;
love be yours and love be mine;

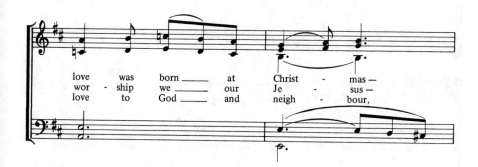

love was born at Christ - mas —
wor - ship we our Je - sus —
love to God and neigh - bour,

star and an - gels gave the sign.
what shall be our sa - cred sign?
love for prayer and gift and sign.

Music: R O Morris (1886-1948)
© Oxford University Press

Words: C Rossetti (1830-1894)
© in this version Jubilate Hymns †

166   Had he not loved us

Beacon Hill

1 Had he not loved us he had nev-er come, yet is he love ___ and love is all his way; low to the mys-tery of the vir-gin's womb ___ Christ bows his glo - ry — born on Christ - mas Day.

2 Had he not loved us he had nev-er come; had he not come ___ he need have nev - er died nor won the vic-tory of the va - cant tomb, ___ the aw - ful tri - umph of the Cru - ci - fied.

3 Had he not loved us he had nev-er come; still were we lost ___ in sor - row, sin and shame, the doors fast shut on our e - ter - nal home ___ which now stand o - pen — for he loved and came.

He comes to us

He comes to us

UNISON

1 He comes to us as one un - known, a
2 He comes when souls in si - lence lie and
3 He comes to us in sound of seas, the

breath un - seen, un - heard; as though with - in a
thoughts of day de - part; half seen up - on the
o - cean's fume and foam; yet small and still up -

heart of stone, or shriv - elled seed in
in - ward eye, a fall - ing star a -
- on the breeze, a wind that stirs the

dark - ness sown, a pulse of be - ing stirred.
- cross the sky of night with - in the heart.
tops of trees, a voice to call us home.

4 He comes in love as once he came
  by flesh and blood and birth;
to bear within our mortal frame
a life, a death, a saving Name,
  for every child of earth.

5 He comes in truth when faith is grown;
  believed, obeyed, adored:
the Christ in all the Scriptures shown,
as yet unseen, but not unknown,
  our Saviour and our Lord.

168 The God we seek

Jesus is born

1 The God we __ seek, be-yond all thought, has now his __ Christ-mas won-der wrought: be-hold, the __ seek-er is the sought! __ Wait-ing end-ed, man be-friend-ed: Je - sus is born!

2 Love is the man-ger where he lies, __ love is the cross on which he dies; __ strong-er than death shall love a-rise! __ Glo-rious meek-ness, power in weak-ness: Je - sus is born!

3 In-to the love of Christ the king our lives, our __ world, in faith we bring: the sin, the __ pain, the suf-fer-ing. __ God es-teems us, Christ re-deems us: Je - sus is born!

Music: © Tom Cunningham †

I wonder as I wander

I wonder as I wander

I

wonder as I wander, out
Jesus was born—it was
Jesus had wanted for
wonder as I wander, out

under the sky, ____ why Jesus the saviour came
in a cow's stall ____ came angels and shepherds and
any one thing ____ a star in the sky, or a
under the sky, ____ why Jesus the Saviour came

down from on high for us lowly people, to suffer and die — I
wise men and all, and from the high heaven a star's light did fall, the
bird on the wing, or all of God's angels in heaven to sing — he
down from on high for us lowly people, to suffer and die — I

wonder as I wander, out under the sky. 2 When
wonderful ____ promise of God to recall. 3 If
surely could ____ have it, for he was the king. 4 I
wonder as I wander, out under the sky.

Music: Appalachian melody
© arranged John Barnard †

Words: Appalachian carol
© in this version Word & Music †

170   **Rejoice and sing**

From *Christmas Oratorio*

Music: J S Bach (1685-1750)

Words: from the German
J Troutbeck (1832-1899)

Before the heaven and earth   171
(Munden)

Munden

UNISON
VOICES

Flowing

1 Be - fore the heaven and earth were made by God's de -
2 Though in the form of God and rich be-yond com -
3 From heights of heaven he came to this world full of
4 The Son be - came true Man and took a ser - vant's
5 O - bed - ient to his death — that death up - on a
6 To him en - throned on high, by an - gel hosts a -

PIANO
or
ORGAN

vv 1-5

- cree, the Son of God all - glor - ious dwelt in God's e - ter - ni - ty.
- pare, he did not stay to grasp his prize; nor did he lin - ger there.
sin, to meet with hun - ger, ha - tred, hell, our life, our love to win.
role; with low - li - ness and self - less love he came, to make us whole.
cross, no son had ev - er shown such love, nor fa - ther known such loss.
- dored, all knees shall

vv 1-5

v 6

bow, and tongues con -fess that Je - sus Christ is Lord.

v 6

Words: from Philippians 2
The Song of Christ's Glory
© Brian Black and Word & Music †

Music: © David Peacock †

172 Before the heaven and earth
(Narenza)

Narenza

1 Be - fore the heaven and earth were
2 Though in the form of God and
3 From heights of heaven he came to

made by God's de - cree, the Son of God all -
rich be - yond com - pare, he did not stay to
this world full of sin, to meet with hun - ger,

- glo - rious dwelt in God's e - ter - ni - ty.
grasp his prize; nor did he lin - ger there.
ha - tred, hell, our did he life, our love to win.

4 The Son became true Man
and took a servant's role;
with lowliness and selfless love
he came, to make us whole.

5 Obedient to his death —
that death upon a cross,
no son had ever shown such love,
nor father known such loss.

6 To him enthroned on high, by angel hosts adored, all knees shall bow, and tongues confess that Jesus Christ is Lord.

Music: adapted from J Leisentritt,
Catholicum Hymnologium (1584)
arranged W H Havergal (1793-1870)
© verse 6 arranged with descant John Barnard †

173   Down from the height
(Purpose)

Purpose

UNISON

1 Down from the height of his glo - ry he came,
2 All through those days his re - solve was the same —
3 Now God has grant - ed him hon - our and fame,

will - ing - ly leav - ing his right - ful do - main:
Je - sus the ser - vant, the shar - er of pain:
ta - ken him up to the high - est to reign:

Je - sus was made in the im - age of man;
per - fect o - be - dience, the path of dis - dain,
'Je - sus is Lord!' ev - ery voice shall main - tain,

love was his mo - tive, and mer - cy his aim.
down to a death of de - ri - sion and shame.
all of cre - a - tion shall bow to his name.

Music: Noël Tredinnick †

Words: from Philippians 2
The Song of Christ's Glory
© Michael Perry †

Down from the height

(Slane)

174

Slane

1 Down from the ___ height of his ___ glo - ry he came,
2 All through those ___ days his re - solve was the same —
3 Now God has ___ grant - ed him ___ hon - our and fame,

will - ing - ly leav - ing his right - ful do - main:
Je - sus the ser - vant, the shar - er of pain:
ta - ken him up to the high - est to reign:

Je - sus ___ was ___ made in the im - age of man; ___
per - fect ___ o - be - dience, the path of dis - dain, ___
'Je - sus ___ is ___ Lord!' ev - ery voice shall main - tain, ___

love was his mo - tive, and ___ mer - cy his aim.
down to a death ___ of de - ri - sion and shame.
all of cre - a - tion shall ___ bow to his name.

Music: Irish traditional melody
arranged M Shaw (1875-1958) altered
© arrangement Oxford University Press

Words: from Philippians 2
The Song of Christ's Glory
© Michael Perry †

175   Behold, the great Creator
(Kilmarnock)

Kilmarnock

1 Behold, the great Creator makes himself a house of clay;— a robe of human form he takes, for ever from this day.

2 Hear this! — the wise eternal Word as Mary's infant cries; — a servant is our mighty Lord, and God in cradle lies.

3 Glad shepherds run to view this sight, a choir of angels sings; — wise men from far with pure delight adore the King of kings.

4 These wonders all the world amaze
and shake the starry frame;
the host of heaven stand to gaze,
and bless the Saviour's name.

5 Join then, all hearts that are not stone,
and all our voices prove
to celebrate the holy one,
the God of peace and love.

Music: N Dougall (1776-1862)

Words: T Pestel (c 1585-1660)
© in this version Jubilate Hymns †

Behold, the great Creator

(This endris nyght)

176

This endris nyght

ORGAN

f

UNISON

f 1 Be - hold, the great Cre - a - tor makes him -
ff 4 These won - ders all the world a - maze and

- self a house of clay; a robe of hu - man
shake the star - ry frame; the host of hea - ven

after verse 4 to
last two pages for verse 5

form he takes for ev - er from this day.
stand to gaze, and bless the Sav- iour's name.

p 2 Hear this! ___ the wise ___ e - ter - nal Word ___ as

Ma - ry's in - fant cries; _____ a ser - vant is ___ our

in - fant, in - fant cries;

might - y Lord, ___ and God ___ in cra - dle lies. _____

DESCANT

f 3 Glad shep - herds run to view this sight, a

MELODY

choir of an - gels sings;_____ wise men from far __ with

back to first page
for verse 4

pure de - light __ a - dore __ the King__ of kings. _____

King of

al - le - lu - ia, al - le - lu - ia,

to ce - le - brate the ho - ly one, the

rit.

al - le - lu - ia, al - le - lu - ia!

rit.

God of peace and love.

rit.

A simpler arrangement of this tune (with other words) appears at number 91.

Music: fifteenth-century English melody
© arranged David Nield †

Words: T Pestel (c 1585-1660)
© in this version Jubilate Hymns †

Good King Wenceslas

Tempus adest floridum

1 ALL Good King Wen - ces - las looked out on the Feast of
2 KING 'Hi - ther, page, and stand by me! if thou know'st it,
3 KING 'Bring me flesh, and bring me wine, bring me pine logs

Ste - phen, when the snow lay round a - bout, deep, and crisp, and
tel - ling. Yon - der poor man — who is he, where and what his
hi - ther: thou and I will see him dine, when we bear them.

e - ven: bright - ly shone the moon that night,
dwell - ing?' PAGE 'Sire, he lives a good league hence,
thi - ther.' ALL Page and mon - arch forth they went,

though the frost was cru - el, when a poor man
un - der - neath the moun - tain; right a - gainst the
forth they went to - ge -- ther, through the wild wind's

came in sight,   ga-thering win - ter   fu - el.'
for - est fence   by Saint Ag - nes'   foun - tain.'
loud la - ment,   and the bit - ter   wea - ther.

PAGE

4 'Sire, the night is darker now,
    and the wind blows stronger;
    fails my heart, I know not how —
    I can go no longer.'

KING

   'Mark my footsteps, good my page,
    tread thou in them boldly:
   thou shalt find the winter's rage
    freeze thy blood less coldly.'

ALL

5 In his master's steps he trod
    where the snow lay even,
   strong to do the will of God
    in the hope of heaven:
   therefore, Christians all, be sure,
    grace and wealth possessing,
   ye who now will bless the poor
    shall yourselves find blessing.

Music: English traditional melody
arranged J Stainer (1840-1901)

Words: J M Neale (1818-1866)
© in this version Word & Music †

178 A song was heard at Christmas

Holy Apostles

PIANO
or
ORGAN

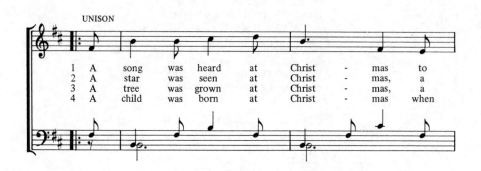

UNISON

1 A song was heard at Christ - mas to
2 A star was seen at Christ - mas, a
3 A tree was grown at Christ - mas, a
4 A child was born at Christ - mas when

wake the mid - night sky; a
her - ald and a sign, that
sap - ling green and young; no
Christ - mas first be - gan; the

sav - iour's birth, and peace on earth, and praise to God on
all might know the way to go to find the child di -
tin - sel bright with can - dle - light up - on its branch - es
Lord of all a ba - by small, the Son of God made

high.   The an - gels sang   at Christ - mas with
- vine.   The wise men watched   at Christ - mas in
hung.   But he who came   at Christ - mas our
man.   For love is ours   at Christ - mas, and

all   the   hosts   a   -   bove,   and
some   far   east   - ern   land,   and
sins   and   sor   -   rows   bore,   and
life   and   light   re -   stored,   and

still   we   sing   the   new - born King, his
still   the   wise   in   star - ry   skies dis -
still   we   name   his   tree   of   shame our
so   we   praise   through end - less days   the

glo - ry   and   his   love.
- cern their Ma - ker's   hand.
life   for ev - er - more.
Sav - iour, Christ the   Lord.

Music: © David Wilson †   Words: © Timothy Dudley-Smith

179   **How joyful is the song**

Venice

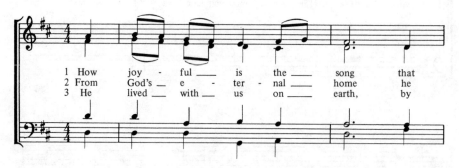

1 How joy - ful __ is the __ song that
2 From God's __ e - ter - nal __ home he
3 He lived __ with __ us on __ earth, by

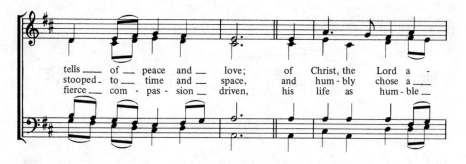

tells __ of __ peace and __ love; of Christ, the Lord a -
stooped _ to __ time and __ space, and hum - bly chose a __
fierce __ com - pas - sion __ driven, his life as hum - ble __

- wait - ed long, de - scend - ing __ from a - bove!
vir - gin's womb to be his __ dwel - ling - place.
as his birth, to show the __ way to __ heaven.

4 And lowlier, in the tomb
  he did not scorn to lie,
  that we frail mortals might assume
  his immortality.

5 How joyful is the song
  that tells of peace and love;
  of Christ, the Lord awaited long,
  descending from above!

Words: after J B de Santeuil (1630-1697)
R Campbell (1814-1868)
© in this version Word & Music †

Music: W Amps (1824-1910)

O Babe divine

O Babe divine

1 O __ Babe __ di - vine, __ to __ you __ we sing __ a __
2 O __ ho - ly Child, __ O __ sight __ su - preme, __ our __
3 O __ Prince __ of peace, __ our __ dark __ world's light, __ the __

Christ - mas song of __ love - long - ing: __ now
pre - sent song, __ our __ fu - ture __ theme: __ as
dawn __ of day, __ the __ end __ of __ night: __ now

make __ our __ hearts __ a __ fer - vent __ spring __ to __
you __ were __ born __ in __ Beth - le - hem, __ be __
give __ us __ strength __ to __ win __ the __ fight = __ to __

love __ you __ more than ev - ery - thing.
born __ in __ us and be __ our __ dream.
con - quer __ sin and live __ a - right.

4 O kingly Christ, our Lord confessed,
prepare your church to love you best;
to live and serve at your behest
in north and south and east and west.

5 O Saviour Jesus, grant us too
the proof of grace, the heavenly view;
come, fill our hearts with love anew
that we may rise to live with you!

Music: C E Pettman (1866-1943)
© 1961 H Freeman and Co.
Reproduced by permission of EMI Publishing Limited and
International Music Publications

Words: traditional
© in this version Word & Music †

181   Jesus, good above all other

Quem pastores laudavere

1 Je - sus, good a - bove __ all o - ther,
2 Je - sus, cra - dled in __ a man - ger,
3 Je - sus, for your peo - ple dy - ing,
4 Lord, in all our do - ings guide __ us:

gen - tle child __ of gen - tle mo - ther;
keep __ us free __ from sin and dan - ger;
ri - sen mas - ter, death de - fy - ing;
pride __ and hate __ shall not di - vide us;

in a sta - ble born __ our bro - ther,
and to all, both friend __ and stran - ger,
Lord of heaven, your grace __ sup - ply - ing,
we'll go on with you __ be - side us,

whom the an - gel hosts __ a - dore:
give your bless - ing ev - er - more.
come to us __ be pre - sent here!
and with joy __ we'll per - se - vere.

Music: fourteenth-century German melody
arranged R Vaughan Williams (1872-1958)
© arrangement Oxford University Press

Words: from the Latin (twelfth century)
J M Neale (1818-1866) verses 1 and 2
P Dearmer (1867-1936) verses 3 and 4
© Oxford University Press

Thank you, God, for Mary's child 182

Joëlle

1 Thank you, God, for Mary's child com - ing like the ris-ing sun,
2 Thank you, God, for each new birth: each new per-son in our hands,
3 God for - give us— we have made such a cha - os of the earth

with new pro - mise and fresh hope cho - rus-ing his match-less dawn.
whose de - pen-dence speaks for you, re - as-serts your love's de - mands.
that an - xi - e - ty and fear mar the mir - a - cle of birth.

4 God, forgive our Babel sounds,
lust for power, religious strife,
breaking fellowship and peace,
sapping all the joy of life.

5 Speak to us in every child,
teach us true humility;
keep our hope alive, sustain
love for all humanity.

6 Till in resurrection light,
peace restored and conflict stilled,
Christ will rise and shine for us,
all his promises fulfilled.

You were a child of mine

Joseph's Carol

UNISON
VOICES

PIANO
or
ORGAN

1 You were a child of mine: ___ I
2 You were a boy of mine: ___ you
3 You were a youth of mine: ___ quite
4 You were a son of mine, ___ full -
5 You are the Lord of all ___ my

watched you born, and wept with joy to see your in - fant
wal - lowed in the sand; you co - pied me at work, and
sud - den - ly you grew, you sought and ques - tioned wi - ser
- grown, my hope and pride; you went your puzz - ling way, a
child, my man, my son; you loved and gave your - self for

head; ___ I held you in my arms, ___
played ___ with ham - mer, wood and nails; ___
men; ___ I felt you break - ing free ___
man ___ so rea - dy, fine and young ___
me. ___ Now I be - long to you; ___

I watched you, awe - struck, as you slept.___ I
you talked to me, and held my hand.___ I
I raged, ad - mired, and feared for you.___ I
life broke in me the day you died.___ I
new worlds are born, new life be - gun.___ I

love you, Son of God: _____ you were a
love you, Son of God: _____ you were a
love you, Son of God: _____ you were a
love you, Son of God: _____ you were a
love you, Son of God: _____ you are the

child _____ of mine. _____
boy _____ of mine. _____
youth _____ of mine. _____
son _____ of mine. _____
Lord _____ of all. _____

Music: E Routley (1917-1982)
© Oxford University Press

Words: Brian Wren
© Oxford University Press

184 No frightened shepherds now

Colwall

1 No fright - ened shep - herds now to stand a -
2 No wood - en man - ger - bed, where we may
3 No choirs of an - gels now to fill a
4 No East - ern Ma - gi here, no gold or

- mazed and quake with fear; but we, sur - prised by
kneel in si - lent awe; yet now we kneel in
star - lit Christ - mas sky; yet, East to West, there
frank - in - cense or myrrh; yet each as pre - cious

joy, come will - ing - ly to Je - sus here.
faith and see, by faith, what an - gels saw.
rings the wor - ship of the Lord most high.
now these hearts of ours as gifts that were.

Music: © David Iliff †

Words: © Paul Wigmore †

GREETING

Welcome, everybody! At Christmas time we delight again to hear the story of the journey to Bethlehem, the song of the angels, the surprise of the shepherds, and their joy as they found Jesus in the manger. But lest we forget he was born to poverty, we remember at this season all who are hungry or cold. And lest we forget he became a refugee, we remember now the stranger and the lonely among us. And lest we forget he felt the pain of life and death, we remember those who are ill, or anxious, or bereaved. And because we know he came for our salvation, let us in heart and mind go once again to Bethlehem, to hear the message of the angels and worship afresh the Son of God.

Editor†

ADVENT SENTENCES

1 Now is the time to wake out of sleep: for now our salvation is nearer than when we first believed. (Romans 13.11)

2 Watch at all times, praying for the strength to stand with confidence before the Son of Man. (Luke 21.36)

3 The kingdom of God is close at hand. Repent, and believe the gospel.
(Mark 1.15)

4 When the Lord comes, he will bring to light things now hidden in darkness, and will disclose the purposes of the heart.
(1 Corinthians 4.5)

5 Our Lord says, Surely I come quickly. Even so: come, Lord Jesus!
(Revelation 22.20)

6 The glory of the Lord shall be revealed: and all mankind shall see it. (Isaiah 40.5)

7 The virgin is with child and will soon give birth to a son: and she will call him Emmanuel, God-is-with-us.
(Isaiah 7.14)

8 In the morning you shall see the glory of the Lord. (Exodus 16.7)

selected for
The Alternative Service Book 1980

CHRISTMAS EVE SENTENCE
(For a 'Midnight' service)

Let the heavens rejoice, and let the earth be glad before the Lord: for he comes!

(1 Chronicles 16.31, 33)

CHRISTMAS SENTENCES

1 The people who walked in darkness have seen a great light: those who dwell in the land of deep darkness, on them has the light shone. (Isaiah 9.2)

2 I bring you news of great joy, a joy to be shared by the whole people: today in the town of David a Saviour has been born to you; he is Christ the Lord. (Luke 2.10)

3 To us a child is born, to us a son is given: and his name will be called the Prince of Peace. (Isaiah 9.6)

4 God's love for us was revealed when God sent his only Son into the world so that we could have life through him. (1 John 4.9)

5 The Word became flesh. He came to dwell among us, and we saw his glory.
(John 1.14)

6 God has shone in our hearts to give the light of the knowledge of his glory in the face of Jesus Christ. (2 Corinthians 4.6)

7 The grace of God has dawned on the world with healing for all mankind.
(Titus 2.11)

selected for
The Alternative Service Book 1980

EPIPHANY SENTENCES

1 Arise, shine, Jerusalem, for your light has come, and the glory of the Lord has risen upon you.   (Isaiah 60.1)

2 From the rising of the sun to its setting my name is great among the nations, says the Lord.   (Malachi 1.11)

3 We have seen his star in the east and have come with gifts to worship the Lord.
(Matthew 2.2)

4 There came a voice from heaven: This is my Son, the Beloved, in whom I am well pleased.   (Matthew 3.17)

5 We have beheld his glory, glory as of the only Son from the Father.   (John 1.14)

selected for
The Alternative Service Book 1980

COLLECTS

1 Almighty God, you make us glad with the yearly remembrance of the birth of your Son Jesus Christ. Grant that, as we joyfully receive him for our redeemer, we may with sure confidence behold him when he shall come to be our judge; who is alive and reigns with you and the Holy Spirit, one God, now and for ever. **Amen**.

Christmas Eve – ASB

2 All praise to you, Almighty God and heavenly king, who sent your Son into the world to take our nature upon him and to be born of a pure virgin. Grant that, as we are born again in him, so he may continually dwell in us and reign on earth as he reigns in heaven with you and the Holy Spirit, now and for ever. **Amen**.

Christmas Day (i) – ASB

3 Eternal God, who made this most holy night to shine with the brightness of your one true light: bring us, who have known the revelation of that light on earth, to see the radiance of your heavenly glory; through Jesus Christ our Lord. **Amen**.

Christmas Day (ii) – ASB

4 Almighty God, who wonderfully created us in your own image and yet more wonderfully restored us through your Son Jesus Christ: grant that, as he came to share in our humanity, so we may share the life of his divinity; who is alive and reigns with you and the Holy Spirit one God, now and for ever. **Amen**.

Christmas 1 (i) – ASB

5 Eternal God, who by the shining of a star led the wise men to the worship of your Son: guide by his light the nations of the earth, that the whole world may behold your glory; through Jesus Christ our Lord. **Amen**.

Christmas 2 (ii)/Epiphany – ASB

6 Almighty God, who anointed Jesus at his baptism with the Holy Spirit and revealed him as your beloved Son: inspire us, your children, who are born of water and the Spirit, to surrender our lives to your service, that we may rejoice to be called the sons of God; through Jesus Christ our Lord. **Amen**.

Epiphany 1 – ASB

© *from The Alternative Service Book*

ADVENT PRAYERS

ABOUT CHRIST'S COMING

O God, who has given us the sure promise that Christ will come to judge the earth: make us ready, we pray, for his royal coming, that we may consider daily what sort of people we ought to be, and as faithful servants wait and work for our Master's return; for his name's sake. **Amen.**

Christopher Idle†

FOR HELP IN BEING READY

Almighty God, our heavenly Father, as we wait for the return of the Lord Jesus Christ, help us to make the best use of the gifts you have given us – our skills, our time and our possessions; help us to share our good things with those in need, as Jesus has taught us to do, and help us to share our faith humbly with those who are not following him, so that they too may be ready when he appears. We ask these things in his name. **Amen.**

Church of St Simon and St Jude, Southsea

ABOUT BEING READY

Lord Jesus Christ, whose advent all shall see: let your coming be with triumph, but not to our shame; let your coming be with glory, but not to our surprise; let your coming be with justice, but not to our judgement. Make our love burn bright for you, our loyalty endure, and our faith increase; that with you we may rejoice on that day, and so enter into your eternal kingdom. **Amen.**

Editor†

FOR HEARTS AND HOMES OPEN TO CHRIST

Loving Father, we thank you for the gift of your Son, whose birth at Bethlehem we now prepare to celebrate: make our hearts and our homes always open to him, that he may dwell with us for ever, and we may serve him gladly all our days, to the honour and glory of your name. **Amen.**

Roger Pickering

ACT OF PRAISE (AT HOLY COMMUNION)

Jesus, you come to live among us, born of the virgin Mary. We give you thanks:
and praise your holy name.

Jesus, you come to us as we read your story in the Bible. We give you thanks:
and praise your holy name.

Jesus, you come to us as we take in faith the bread and wine. We give you thanks:
and praise your holy name.

Jesus, you will come to reign in glory. We give you thanks:
and praise your holy name. Amen. Come, Lord Jesus!

St Catharine's, Houghton on the Hill, Leicester

CHRISTMAS PRAYERS

ACT OF PRAISE

Let us worship the Saviour:

Heavenly king, yet born of Mary; Jesus, Son of God,
we praise and adore you.

Eternal Word, yet child without speech; Jesus, Son of God,
we praise and adore you.

Robed in glory, yet wrapped in infant clothes; Jesus, Son of God,
we praise and adore you.

Lord of heaven and earth, yet laid in a manger; Jesus, Son of God,
we praise and adore you.

To you, O Jesus,
strong in your weakness,
glorious in your humility,
mighty to save,
be all praise and glory,
with the Father and the Holy Spirit,
now and for ever. Amen.

From Worship Now

CONFESSION

We confess that amid all the joys and festivities of this season we have sometimes forgotten what Christmas really means, and have left the Lord Jesus out of our thinking and living:
Father, forgive us.

Help us to remember that you loved the world so much that you gave your only Son, who was born to be our Saviour:
Lord, help us.

We confess that we have allowed the most important event in history to become dulled by familiarity:
Father, forgive us.

Help us in this act of worship to recapture a sense of wonder, and to discover again the stupendous fact that the Creator of the universe has come to us as a newborn baby:
Lord, help us.

We confess to a selfish enjoyment of Christmas while we do little to help the homeless families of your world:
Father, forgive us.

Fill our hearts with the love that cares,
that understands and gives;
show us how we can best serve
those in need;
for the sake of him
who was born in a stable,
Jesus Christ our Lord. Amen.

Copyright information sought

FOR OUR WORLD

O God, we thank you for the message of peace that Christmas brings to our distracted world. Give peace among nations; peace in our lands, peace in our homes, and peace in our hearts, as we remember the birth at Bethlehem of the Prince of peace, Jesus Christ our Lord. **Amen.**

from Worship Now

FOR THOSE WITHOUT FAITH

O Holy Spirit of Christ – teacher, helper, and friend: open the hearts and minds of many this Christmas-time to the good and saving news of Jesus Christ; that those who are insecure, or empty, or aimless, may find in the One from Bethlehem all that they need today, and much more besides; for his name's sake. **Amen.**

Christopher Idle†

THE GREATEST PRESENT

O God our Father, we praise you for Christmas – our happiness and presents, our families and the friends we see again; and for this greatest present of all we thank you: for the gift of Jesus at Bethlehem to be our saviour and our king. **Amen.**

Editor†

CHILDREN'S THANKSGIVING

Heavenly Father, for your forgiving love, **we give you thanks and praise;**

for the beauty of the world around us, **we give you thanks and praise;**

for the love of our parents and our friends, **we give you thanks and praise;**

for work and play, for food and clothes: **we give you thanks and praise;**

for happiness, laughter and fun: **we give you thanks and praise.**

But most of all we thank you for the birth of Jesus Christ, your Son; for the example of his life, for the love that made him die for us, and for your power that raised him from the dead: help us to serve him gladly and faithfully all our days. **Amen.**

Editor†

THANKSGIVING

God our Father, we listen again to the story of Christmas, and we are glad that Jesus has come to be our saviour and our friend.

We hear how Mary laid her baby in a manger. Jesus has come: **thank you, Father.**

We hear how the angels sang over the Bethlehem hills: 'Glory to God; peace for the world.' Jesus has come: **thank you, Father.**

We hear how the shepherds hurried to see that what the angel said was true. Jesus has come: **thank you, Father.**

We hear how the wise men came to bring their worship and their precious gifts. Jesus has come: **thank you, Father.**

O God, we thank you that Jesus has come to be our saviour and our friend: we welcome him with love, and worship him with gladness, for your glory's sake. Amen.

National Christian Education Council

EPIPHANY PRAYERS

CONFESSION

Lord Jesus Christ, wise men from the East worshipped and adored you; they brought you gifts – gold, incense, and myrrh.

We too have seen your glory, but we have often turned away. Lord, in your mercy, **forgive us and help us.**

We too have gifts, but we have not fully used them or offered them to you. Lord, in your mercy, **forgive us and help us.**

We too have acclaimed you as King, but we have not served you with all our strength. Lord, in your mercy, **forgive us and help us.**

We too have acknowledged you as God, but we have not striven for holiness. Lord, in your mercy, **forgive us and help us.**

We too have welcomed you as Saviour, but we have failed to tell others of your love. Lord, in your mercy, **forgive us and help us.**

Make our trust more certain, make our love more true, make our worship more acceptable; for your glory's sake. Amen.

Editor†

FOR THOSE IN NEED

Remember, O merciful God, all those in need: people with no good food or proper clothes, no home of their own or no work to do, no family or friends, or no knowledge of your love. Move us to respond to their plight, and strengthen us to help them; through Jesus Christ, our Lord. **Amen.**

Christopher Idle†

LITANY

Christ, born in a stable, give courage to all who are homeless; in your mercy,
hear our prayer.

Christ, who fled into Egypt, give comfort to all refugees; in your mercy,
hear our prayer.

Christ, who fasted in the desert, give relief to all who are hungry; in your mercy,
hear our prayer.

Christ, who hung in torment on the cross, give your strength to all who suffer; in your mercy,
hear our prayer.

Christ, who died to save us, give us the assurance of your forgiveness; in your mercy,
hear our prayer.

Save us today,
and use us in your loving purposes;
for your glory's sake. Amen.

after Simon Baynes

FOR THE HOMELESS

Lord Jesus Christ, born in a stable: hear the cry of the homeless and refugees, and so move our will by your Holy Spirit that we may not rest content until they have found home and livelihood; for your name's sake. **Amen.**

from New Every Morning

FOR CHILDREN EVERYWHERE

Heavenly Father, whose children suffered at the hands of Herod though they had done no wrong: help us to defend all your children from cruelty and oppression; in the name of Jesus Christ who suffered for us, but is alive and reigns with you and the Holy Spirit, one God, now and for ever. **Amen.**

Holy Innocents Collect – APB

FOR THE MIND OF JESUS

Father of mankind, who gave your only-begotten Son to take upon himself the form of a servant and to be obedient even to death on a cross: give us the same mind that was in Christ Jesus that, sharing his humility, we may come to be with him in his glory; who is alive and reigns with you and the Holy Spirit, one God, now and for ever. **Amen.**

Pentecost 10 – ASB

CHRISTMAS BLESSINGS

1 Christ the Sun of Righteousness shine upon you, and scatter the darkness from before your path; and the blessing of God Almighty, the Father, the Son, and the Holy Spirit, be among you, and remain with you always. **Amen.**

2 Christ, who by his incarnation gathered into one all things earthly and heavenly, fill you with his joy and peace; and the blessing of God Almighty, the Father, the Son, and the Holy Spirit, be among you, and remain with you always. **Amen.**

3 Christ the Son of God, born of Mary, fill you with his grace to trust his promises and obey his will; and the blessing of God Almighty, the Father, the Son, and the Holy Spirit, be among you, and remain with you always. **Amen.**

4 Christ the Son of God gladden your hearts with the good news of his kingdom; and the blessing of God Almighty, the Father, the Son, and the Holy Spirit, be among you, and remain with you always. **Amen.**

from The Alternative Service Book 1980

5 Go in peace: the wisdom of the Wonderful Counsellor guide you, the strength of the Mighty God defend you, the love of the Everlasting Father enfold you, the peace of the Prince of Peace be upon you; and the blessing of God Almighty, the Father, the Son, and the Holy Spirit, be among you, and remain with you always. **Amen.**

from Worship Now

6 The joy of the angels, the wonder of the shepherds, and the peace of the Christ child, fill your hearts this Christmas time; and the blessing of God the Father, God the Son, and God the Holy Spirit, be with you now and always. **Amen.**

Editor†

ADVENT READINGS

CHRISTMAS READINGS

EPIPHANY READINGS

Page

PROCLAIMING THE SAVIOUR

ADVENT READINGS
First Set

GOD'S PROMISE
TO HIS PEOPLE

1 Hear the good news!
(Isaiah 52.7–10: corresponding carols 2–10, 16)

How beautiful on the mountains are the feet of those who bring good news, who proclaim peace, who bring good tidings, who proclaim salvation, who say to Zion, 'Your God reigns!' Listen! Your watchmen lift up their voices; together they shout for joy. When the Lord returns to Zion, they will see it with their own eyes. Burst into songs of joy together, you ruins of Jerusalem, for the Lord has comforted his people, he has redeemed Jerusalem. The Lord will lay bare his holy arm in the sight of all the nations, and all the ends of the earth will see the salvation of our God.

Reader: This is the word of the Lord.
People: Thanks be to God.

2 Proclaim the saviour!
(Isaiah 62.10–12: corresponding carols 6–15)

Pass through, pass through the gates! Prepare the way for the people. Build up, build up the highway! Remove the stones. Raise a banner for the nations.

The Lord has made proclamation to the ends of the earth: Say to the Daughter of Zion, 'See, your Saviour comes! See, his reward is with him, and his recompense accompanies him!' They will be called The Holy People, The Redeemed of the Lord; and you will be called Sought After, The City No Longer Deserted.

Reader: This is the word of the Lord.
People: Thanks be to God.

3 Rejoice at his coming!
(Isaiah 35.1–10: corresponding carol 35)

The desert and the parched land will be glad; the wilderness will rejoice and blossom. Like the crocus, it will burst into bloom; it will rejoice greatly and shout for joy. The glory of Lebanon will be given to it, the splendour of Carmel and Sharon; they will see the glory of the Lord, the splendour of our God.

Strengthen the feeble hands, steady the knees that give way; say to those with fearful hearts, 'Be strong, do not fear; your God will come, he will come with vengeance; with divine retribution he will come to save you.'

Then will the eyes of the blind be opened and the ears of the deaf unstopped. Then will the lame leap like a deer, and the mute tongue shout for joy. Water will gush forth in the wilderness and streams in the desert. The burning sand will become a pool, the thirsty ground bubbling springs. In the haunts where jackals once lay, grass and reeds and papyrus will grow.

And a highway will be there; it will be called the Way of Holiness. The unclean will not journey on it; it will be for those who walk in that Way; wicked fools will not go about on it. No lion will be there, nor will any ferocious beast get up on it; they will not be found there. But only the redeemed will walk there, and the ransomed of the Lord will return. They will enter Zion with singing; everlasting joy will crown their heads. Gladness and joy will overtake them, and sorrow and sighing will flee away.

Reader: This is the word of the Lord.
People: Thanks be to God.

4 Welcome the dawn!
(Isaiah 9.2, 6–7: corresponding carols 20–24)

The people walking in darkness have seen a great light; on those living in the land of the shadow of death a light has dawned. For to us a child is born, to us a son is given, and the government will be on his shoulders. And he will be called Wonderful Counsellor, Mighty God, Everlasting Father, Prince of Peace. Of the increase of his government and peace there will be no end. He will reign on David's throne and over his kingdom, establishing and upholding it with justice and righteousness from that time on and for ever. The zeal of the Lord Almighty will accomplish this.

Reader: This is the word of the Lord.
People: Thanks be to God.

5 Worship the King!
(Psalm 96.1–13: corresponding carols 150)

Sing to the Lord a new song; sing to the Lord, all the earth. Sing to the Lord, praise his name; proclaim his salvation day after day. Declare his glory among the nations, his marvellous deeds among all peoples. For great is the Lord and most worthy of praise; he is to be feared above all gods. For all the gods of the nations are idols, but the Lord made the heavens. Splendour and majesty are before him; strength and glory are in his sanctuary.

Ascribe to the Lord, O families of nations, ascribe to the Lord glory and strength. Ascribe to the Lord the glory due to his name; bring an offering and come into his courts. Worship the Lord in the splendour of his holiness; tremble before him, all the earth.

Say among the nations, 'The Lord reigns.' The world is firmly established, it cannot be moved; he will judge the peoples with equity. Let the heavens rejoice, let the earth be glad; let the sea resound, and all that is in it; let the fields be jubilant, and everything in them. Then all the trees of the forest will sing for joy; they will sing before the Lord, for he comes, he comes to judge the earth. He will judge the world in righteousness and the peoples in his truth.

Reader: This is the word of the Lord.
People: Thanks be to God.

6 Look for the promise!
(Isaiah 11.1–5: corresponding carols 1, 24)

A shoot will come up from the stump of Jesse; from his roots a Branch will bear fruit. The Spirit of the Lord will rest on him – the Spirit of wisdom and of understanding, the Spirit of counsel and of power, the Spirit of knowledge and of the fear of the Lord – and he will delight in the fear of the Lord. He will not judge by what he sees with his eyes, or decide by what he hears with his ears; but with righteousness he will judge the needy, with justice he will give decisions for the poor of the earth. He will strike the earth with the rod of his mouth; with the breath of his lips he will slay the wicked. Righteousness will be his belt and faithfulness the sash round his waist.

Reader: This is the word of the Lord.
People: Thanks be to God.

7 Prepare the way!
(Luke 1.67–70, 76–79: corresponding carol 2)

John the Baptist's father Zechariah was filled with the Holy Spirit and prophesied: 'Praise be to the Lord, the God of Israel, because he has come and has redeemed his people. He has raised up a horn of salvation for us in the house of his servant David – as he said through his holy prophets of long ago. And you, my child, will be called a prophet of the Most High; for you will go on before the Lord to prepare the way for him, to give his people the knowledge of salvation through the forgiveness of their sins, because of the tender mercy of our God, by which the rising sun will come to us from heaven to shine on those living in darkness and in the shadow of death, to guide our feet into the path of peace.'

Reader: This is the word of the Lord.
People: Thanks be to God.

8 Praise the Lord!
(Ephesians 1.3–10: corresponding carols 179–180)

Praise be to the God and Father of our Lord Jesus Christ, who has blessed us in the heavenly realms with every spiritual blessing in Christ. For he chose us in him before the creation of the world to be holy and blameless in his sight. In love he predestined us to be adopted as his sons through Jesus Christ, in accordance with his pleasure and will – to the praise of his glorious grace, which he has freely given us in the One he loves. In him we have redemption through his blood, the forgiveness of sins, in accordance with the riches of God's grace that he lavished on us with all wisdom and understanding. And he made known to us the mystery of his will according to his good pleasure, which he purposed in Christ, to be put into effect when the times will have reached their fulfilment – to bring all things in heaven and on earth together under one head, even Christ.

Reader: This is the word of the Lord.
People: Thanks be to God.

ADVENT READINGS
Second Set

THE HOPE OF SALVATION

1 The people cry out
(Isaiah 64.1–5: corresponding carols 1, 2, 5)

Oh, that you would rend the heavens and come down, that the mountains would tremble before you! As when fire sets twigs ablaze and causes water to boil, come down to make your name known to your enemies and cause the nations to quake before you! For when you did awesome things that we did not expect, you came down, and the mountains trembled before you. Since ancient times no-one has heard, no ear has perceived, no eye has seen any God besides you, who acts on behalf of those who wait for him. You come to the help of those who gladly do right, who remember your ways. But when we continued to sin against them, you were angry. How then can we be saved?

Reader: This is the word of the Lord.
People: Thanks be to God.

2 Some listen to God
(Psalm 85.4–9 : corresponding carol 7)

Restore us again, O God our Saviour, and put away your displeasure towards us. Will you be angry with us for ever? Will you prolong your anger through all generations? Will you not revive us again, that your people may rejoice in you?

Show us your unfailing love, O Lord, and grant us your salvation. I will listen to what God the Lord will say; he promises peace to his people, his saints – but let them not return to folly. Surely his salvation is near those who fear him, that his glory may dwell in our land.

Reader: This is the word of the Lord.
People: Thanks be to God.

3 God comforts his people
(Isaiah 40.1–5: corresponding carol 8)

Comfort, comfort my people, says your God. Speak tenderly to Jerusalem, and proclaim to her that her hard service has been completed, that her sin has been paid for, that she has received from the Lord's hand double for all her sins.

A voice of one calling: 'In the desert prepare the way for the Lord; make straight in the wilderness a highway for our God. Every valley shall be raised up, every mountain and hill made low; the rough ground shall become level, the rugged places a plain. And the glory of the Lord will be revealed, and all mankind together will see it. For the mouth of the Lord has spoken.'

Reader: This is the word of the Lord.
People: Thanks be to God.

4 God promises his messenger
(Malachi 3.1–3: corresponding carol 160)

'See, I will send my messenger, who will prepare the way before me. Then suddenly the Lord you are seeking will come to his temple; the messenger of the covenant, whom you desire, will come,' says the Lord Almighty. But who can endure the day of his coming? Who can stand when he appears? For he will be like a refiner's fire or a launderer's soap. He will sit as a refiner and purifier of silver; he will purify the Levites and refine them like gold and silver.

Reader: This is the word of the Lord.
People: Thanks be to God.

5 God promises a saviour
(Numbers 24.15–17; Jeremiah 23.5–6: corresponding carols 1, 24)

A
The oracle of one whose eye sees clearly, the oracle of one who hears the words of God, who has knowledge from the Most High, who sees a vision from the Almighty, who falls prostrate, and whose eyes are opened: 'I see him, but not now; I behold him, but not near. A star will come out of Jacob; a sceptre will rise out of Israel.'

B
'The days are coming,' declares the Lord, 'when I will raise up to David a righteous Branch, a King who will reign wisely and do what is just and right in the land. In his days Judah will be saved and Israel will live in safety. This is the name by which he will be called: The Lord Our Righteousness.'

Reader: This is the word of the Lord.
People: Thanks be to God.

6 God confirms his love
(Micah 5.2–5a: corresponding carols 17, 91, 134)

'But you, Bethlehem Ephrathah, though you are small among the clans of Judah, out of you will come for me one who will be ruler over Israel, whose origins are from of old, from ancient times.'

Therefore Israel will be abandoned until the time when she who is in labour gives birth and the rest of his brothers return to join the Israelites.

He will stand and shepherd his flock in the strength of the Lord, in the majesty of the name of the Lord his God. And they will live securely, for then his greatness will reach to the ends of the earth. And he will be their peace.

Reader: This is the word of the Lord.
People: Thanks be to God.

7 God declares his coming
(Zechariah 2.10–13: corresponding carols 12–15)

'Shout and be glad, O Daughter of Zion. For I am coming, and I will live among you,' declares the Lord. 'Many nations will be joined with the Lord in that day and will become my people. I will live among you and you will know that the Lord Almighty has sent me to you. The Lord will inherit Judah as his portion in the holy land and will again choose Jerusalem. Be still before the Lord, all mankind, because he has roused himself from his holy dwelling.'

Reader: This is the word of the Lord.
People: Thanks be to God.

8 We wait for his appearing
(Titus 2.11–14, 3.3–7: corresponding carols 9–11, 18–19)

The grace of God that brings salvation has appeared to all men. It teaches us to say 'No' to ungodliness and worldly passions, and to live self-controlled, upright and godly lives in this present age, while we wait for the blessed hope – the glorious appearing of our great God and Saviour, Jesus Christ, who gave himself for us to redeem us from all wickedness and to purify for himself a people that are his very own, eager to do what is good.

At one time we too were foolish, disobedient, deceived and enslaved by all kinds of passions and pleasures. We lived in malice and envy, being hated and hating one another. But when the kindness and love of God our Saviour appeared, he saved us, not because of righteous things we had done, but because of his mercy. He saved us through the washing of rebirth and renewal by the Holy Spirit, whom he poured out on us generously through Jesus Christ our Saviour, so that, having been justified by his grace, we might become heirs having the hope of eternal life.

Reader: This is the word of the Lord.
People: Thanks be to God.

ADVENT READINGS
Third Set

THE COMING LORD

1 Luke begins his Gospel
(Luke 1.1–4: corresponding carol 19)

Many have undertaken to draw up an account of the things that have been fulfilled among us, just as they were handed down to us by those who from the first were eye-witnesses and servants of the word. Therefore, since I myself have carefully investigated everything from the beginning, it seemed good also to me to write an orderly account for you, most excellent Theophilus, so that you may know the certainty of the things you have been taught.

Reader: This is the word of the Lord.
People: Thanks be to God.

2 John the Baptist's parents are told
(Luke 1.5–8, 11–17: corresponding carol 160)

In the time of Herod king of Judea there was a priest named Zechariah, who belonged to the priestly division of Abijah; his wife Elizabeth was also a descendant of Aaron. Both of them were upright in the sight of God, observing all the Lord's commandments and regulations blamelessly. But they had no children, because Elizabeth was barren; and they were both well on in years. Once when Zechariah was serving as priest before God, an angel of the Lord appeared to him, standing at the right side of the altar of incense. When Zechariah saw him, he was startled and was gripped with fear. But the angel said to him: 'Do not be afraid, Zechariah; your prayer has been heard. Your wife Elizabeth will bear you a son, and you are to give him the name

John. He will be a joy and delight to you, and many will rejoice because of his birth, for he will be great in the sight of the Lord. He is never to take wine or other fermented drink, and he will be filled with the Holy Spirit even from birth. Many of the people of Israel will he bring back to the Lord their God. And he will go on before the Lord, in the spirit and power of Elijah, to turn the hearts of the fathers to their children and the disobedient to the wisdom of the righteous – to make ready a people prepared for the Lord.'

Reader: This is the word of the Lord.
People: Thanks be to God.

3 Zechariah finds it hard to believe
(Luke 1.18–25: corresponding carols 7, 8)

Zechariah asked the angel, 'How can I be sure of this? I am an old man and my wife is well on in years.' The angel answered, 'I am Gabriel. I stand in the presence of God, and I have been sent to speak to you and to tell you this good news. And now you will be silent and not able to speak until the day this happens, because you did not believe my words, which will come true at their proper time.' Meanwhile, the people were waiting for Zechariah and wondering why he stayed so long in the temple. When he came out, he could not speak to them. They realised he had seen a vision in the temple, for he kept making signs to them but remained unable to speak. When his time of service was completed, he returned home. After this his wife Elizabeth became pregnant and for five months remained in seclusion. 'The Lord has done this for me,' she said. 'In these days he has shown his favour and taken away my disgrace among the people.'

Reader: This is the word of the Lord.
People: Thanks be to God.

4 Mary is told about Jesus
(Luke 1.26–38: corresponding carols 25–27)

In the sixth month, God sent the angel Gabriel to Nazareth, a town in Galilee, to a virgin pledged to be married to a man named Joseph, a descendant of David. The virgin's name was Mary. The angel went to her and said, 'Greetings, you who are highly favoured! The Lord is with you.' Mary was greatly troubled at his words and wondered what kind of greeting this might be. But the angel said to her, 'Do not be afraid, Mary, you have found favour with God. You will be with child and give birth to a son, and you are to give him the name Jesus. He will be great and will be called the Son of the Most High. The Lord God will give him the throne of his father David, and he will reign over the house of Jacob for ever; his kingdom will never end.' 'How will this be,' Mary asked the angel, 'since I am a virgin?' The angel answered, 'The Holy Spirit will come upon you, and the power of the Most High will overshadow you. So the holy one to be born will be called the Son of God. Even Elizabeth your relative is going to have a child in her old age, and she who was said to be barren is in her sixth month. For nothing is impossible with God.' 'I am the Lord's servant,' Mary answered. 'May it be to me as you have said.' Then the angel left her.

Reader: This is the word of the Lord.
People: Thanks be to God.

5 Mary visits Elizabeth

(Luke 1.39–45: corresponding carols 28–29)

At that time Mary got ready and hurried to a town in the hill country of Judea, where she entered Zechariah's home and greeted Elizabeth. When Elizabeth heard Mary's greeting, the baby leaped in her womb, and Elizabeth was filled with the Holy Spirit. In a loud voice she exclaimed: 'Blessed are you among women, and blessed is the child you will bear! But why am I so favoured, that the mother of my Lord should come to me? As soon as the sound of your greeting reached my ears, the baby in my womb leaped for joy. Blessed is she who has believed that what the Lord has said to her will be accomplished!'

Reader: This is the word of the Lord.
People: Thanks be to God.

6 John the Baptist is born

(Luke 1.57–66: corresponding carols 12, 20–22)

When it was time for Elizabeth to have her baby, she gave birth to a son. Her neighbours and relatives heard that the Lord had shown her great mercy, and they shared her joy. On the eighth day they came to circumcise the child, and they were going to name him after his father Zechariah, but his mother spoke up and said, 'No! He is to be called John.'

They said to her, 'There is no-one among your relatives who has that name.' Then they made signs to his father, to find out what he would like to name the child. He asked for a writing tablet, and to everyone's astonishment he wrote, 'His name is John.' Immediately his mouth was opened and his tongue was loosed, and he began to speak, praising God. The neighbours were all filled with awe, and throughout the hill country of Judea people were talking about all these things. Everyone who heard this wondered about it, asking, 'What then is this child going to be?' For the Lord's hand was with him.

Reader: This is the word of the Lord.
People: Thanks be to God.

7 God's purpose is explained to Joseph

(Matthew 1.18–25: corresponding carols 30–31, 33, 95)

This is how the birth of Jesus Christ came about: His mother Mary was pledged to be married to Joseph, but before they came together, she was found to be with child through the Holy Spirit. Because Joseph her husband was a righteous man and did not want to expose her to public disgrace, he had in mind to divorce her quietly. But after he had considered this, an angel of the Lord appeared to him in a dream and said, 'Joseph son of David, do not be afraid to take Mary home as your wife, because what is conceived in her is from the Holy Spirit. She will give birth to a son, and you are to give him the name Jesus, because he will save his people from their sins.' All this took place to fulfil what the Lord had said through the prophet: 'The virgin will be with child and will give birth to a son, and they will call him Immanuel' – which means, 'God with us'. When Joseph woke up, he did what the angel of the Lord had commanded him and took Mary home as his wife. But he had no union with her until she gave birth to a son. And he gave him the name Jesus.

Reader: This is the word of the Lord.
People: Thanks be to God.

8 The Lord is near
(Philippians 4.4–9: corresponding carols 70–75)

Rejoice in the Lord always. I will say it again: Rejoice! Let your gentleness be evident to all. The Lord is near. Do not be anxious about anything, but in everything, by prayer and petition, with thanksgiving, present your requests to God. And the peace of God, which transcends all understanding, will guard your hearts and your minds in Christ Jesus. Finally, brothers, whatever is true, whatever is noble, whatever is right, whatever is pure, whatever is lovely, whatever is admirable – if anything is excellent or praiseworthy – think about such things. Whatever you have learned or received or heard from me, or seen in me – put it into practice. And the God of peace will be with you.

Reader: This is the word of the Lord.
People: Thanks be to God.

CHRISTMAS READINGS
First Set

THE LIGHT OF THE WORLD

1 Let there be light!
(Genesis 1.1–5: corresponding carols 3, 23, 101)

In the beginning God created the heavens and the earth. Now the earth was formless and empty, darkness was over the surface of the deep, and the Spirit of God was hovering over the waters.

And God said, 'Let there be light,' and there was light. God saw that the light was good, and he separated the light from the darkness. God called the light 'day', and the darkness he called 'night'. And there was evening and there was morning – the first day.

Reader: This is the word of the Lord.
People: Thanks be to God.

2 Light in the darkness
(John 1.1–9: corresponding carols 19, 75, 81–82, 100, 163, 167)

In the beginning was the Word, and the Word was with God, and the Word was God. He was with God in the beginning. Through him all things were made; without him nothing was made that has been made. In him was life, and that life was the light of men. The light shines in the darkness, but the darkness has not understood it. There came a man who was sent from God; his name was John. He came as a witness to testify concerning that light, so that through him all men might believe. He himself was not the light; he came only as a witness to the light. The true light that gives light to every man was coming into the world.

Reader: This is the word of the Lord.
People: Thanks be to God.

3 Light in the shadow of death
(Isaiah 9.2, 6–7: corresponding carols 20–24)

The people walking in darkness have seen a great light; on those living in the land of the shadow of death a light has dawned. For to us a child is born, to us a son is given, and the government will be on his shoulders. And he will be called Wonderful Counsellor, Mighty God, Everlasting Father, Prince of Peace. Of the increase of his government and peace there will be no end. He will reign on David's throne and over his kingdom, establishing and upholding it with justice and righteousness from that time on and for ever. The zeal of the Lord Almighty will accomplish this.

Reader: This is the word of the Lord.
People: Thanks be to God.

4 The Sun will rise
(Luke 1.67–70, 76–79: corresponding carol 2)

John the Baptist's father Zechariah was filled with the Holy Spirit and prophesied: 'Praise be to the Lord, the God of Israel, because he has come and has redeemed his people. He has raised up a horn of salvation for us in the house of his servant David – as he said through his holy prophets of long ago. And you, my child, will be called a prophet of the Most High; for you will go on before the Lord to prepare the way for him, to give his people the knowledge of salvation through the forgiveness of their sins, because of the tender mercy of our God, by which the rising sun will come to us from heaven to shine on those living in darkness and in the shadow of death, to guide our feet into the path of peace.'

Reader: This is the word of the Lord.
People: Thanks be to God.

5 Light comes into the world
(Luke 2.1–7: corresponding carols 32–76)

In those days Caesar Augustus issued a decree that a census should be taken of the entire Roman world. This was the first census that took place while Quirinius was governor of Syria. And everyone went to his own town to register. So Joseph also went up from the town of Nazareth in Galilee to Judea, to Bethlehem the town of David, because he belonged to the house and line of David. He went there to register with Mary, who was pledged to be married to him and was expecting a child. While they were there, the time came for the baby to be born, and she gave birth to her firstborn, a son. She wrapped him in strips of cloth and placed him in a manger, because there was no room for them in the inn.

Reader: This is the word of the Lord.
People: Thanks be to God.

6 Light fills the skies
(Luke 2.8–14: corresponding carols 77–107)

And there were shepherds living out in the fields near by, keeping watch over their flocks at night. An angel of the Lord appeared to them, and the glory of the Lord shone around them, and they were terrified. But the angel said to them, 'Do not be afraid. I bring you good news of great joy that will be for all the people. Today in the town of David a Saviour has been born to you; he is Christ the Lord. This will be a sign to you: You will find a baby wrapped in strips of cloth and lying in a manger.' Suddenly a great company of the heavenly host appeared with the angel, praising God and saying, 'Glory to God in the highest, and on earth peace to men on whom his favour rests.'

Reader: This is the word of the Lord.
People: Thanks be to God.

7 Give praise for the light!
(Luke 2.15–20: corresponding carols 108–129)

When the angels had left them and gone into heaven, the shepherds said to one another, 'Let's go to Bethlehem and see this thing that has happened, which the Lord has told us about.' So they hurried off and found Mary and Joseph, and the baby, who was lying in the manger. When they had seen him, they spread the word concerning what had been told them about this child, and all who heard it were amazed at what the shepherds said to them. But Mary treasured up all these things and pondered them in her heart. The shepherds returned, glorifying and praising God for all the things they had heard and seen, which were just as they had been told.

Reader: This is the word of the Lord.
People: Thanks be to God.

8 Follow the light!
(Matthew 2.1–2, 8–11: corresponding carols 130–153; 158–159)

After Jesus was born in Bethlehem in Judea, during the time of King Herod, Magi from the east came to Jerusalem and asked, 'Where is the one who has been born king of the Jews? We saw his star in the east and have come to worship him.' Herod sent them to Bethlehem and said, 'Go and make a careful search for the child. As soon as you find him, report to me, so that I too may go and worship him.' After they had heard the king, they went on their way, and the star they had seen in the east went ahead of them until it stopped over the place where the child was. When they saw the star, they were overjoyed. On coming to the house, they saw the child with his mother Mary, and they bowed down and worshipped him. Then they opened their treasures and presented him with gifts of gold and of incense and of myrrh.

Reader: This is the word of the Lord.
People: Thanks be to God.

9 The light of God's glory
(Hebrews 1.1–3: corresponding carols 21–23, 72, 75)

In the past God spoke to our forefathers through the prophets at many times and in various ways, but in these last days he has spoken to us by his Son, whom he appointed heir of all things, and through whom he made the universe. The Son is the radiance of God's glory and the exact representation of his being, sustaining all things by his powerful word. After he had provided purification for sins, he sat down at the right hand of the Majesty in heaven.

Reader: This is the word of the Lord.
People: Thanks be to God.

10 The light is acclaimed
(Luke 2.25–32: corresponding carols 154–157)

Now there was a man in Jerusalem called Simeon, who was righteous and devout. He was waiting for the consolation of Israel, and the Holy Spirit was upon him. It had been revealed to him by the Holy Spirit that he would not die before he had seen the Lord's Christ. Moved by the Spirit, he went into the temple courts. When the parents brought in the child Jesus to do for him what the custom of the Law required, Simeon took him in his arms and praised God, saying: 'Sovereign Lord, as you have promised, you now dismiss your servant in peace. For my eyes have seen your salvation, which you have prepared in the sight of all people, a light for revelation to the Gentiles and for glory to your people Israel.'

Reader: This is the word of the Lord.
People: Thanks be to God.

11 The light shines in our hearts
(2 Corinthians 4.2–6: corresponding carols 35–38, 59, 80)

By setting forth the truth plainly we commend ourselves to every man's conscience in the sight of God. And even if our gospel is veiled, it is veiled to those who are perishing. The god of this age has blinded the minds of unbelievers, so that they cannot see the light of the gospel of the glory of Christ, who is the image of God. For we do not preach ourselves, but Jesus Christ as Lord, and ourselves as your servants for Jesus' sake. For God, who said, 'Let light shine out of darkness,' made his light shine in our hearts to give us the light of the knowledge of the glory of God in the face of Christ.

Reader: This is the word of the Lord.
People: Thanks be to God.

CHRISTMAS READINGS
Second Set

GOOD NEWS FOR THE PEOPLE

1 The people have a hope
(Psalm 85.4–11: corresponding carol 7)

Restore us again, O God our Saviour, and put away your displeasure towards us. Will you be angry with us for ever? Will you prolong your anger through all generations? Will you not revive us again, that your people may rejoice in you? Show us your unfailing love, O Lord, and grant us your salvation. I will listen to what God the Lord will say; he promises peace to his people, his saints – but let them not return to folly. Surely his salvation is near those who fear him, that his glory may dwell in our land. Love and faithfulness meet together; righteousness and peace kiss each other. Faithfulness springs forth from the earth, and righteousness looks down from heaven.

Reader: This is the word of the Lord.
People: Thanks be to God.

2 The people have a saviour
(Luke 2.8–18: corresponding carols 84–129)

There were shepherds living out in the fields near Bethlehem, keeping watch over their flocks at night. An angel of the Lord appeared to them, and the glory of the Lord shone around them, and they were terrified. But the angel said to them, 'Do not be afraid. I bring you good news of great joy that will be for all the people. Today in the town of David a Saviour has been born to you; he is Christ the Lord. This will be a sign to you: You will find a baby wrapped in strips of cloth and lying in a manger.' Suddenly a great company of the heavenly host appeared with the angel, praising God and saying, 'Glory to God in the highest, and on earth peace to men on whom his favour rests.' When the angels had left them and gone into heaven, the shepherds said to one another, 'Let's go to Bethlehem and see this thing that has happened, which the Lord has told us about.' So they hurried off and found Mary and Joseph, and the baby, who was lying in the manger. When they had seen him, they spread the word concerning what had been told them about this child, and all who heard it were amazed at what the shepherds said to them.

Reader: This is the word of the Lord.
People: Thanks be to God.

3 Some have rejected him
(Isaiah 53.1–3: corresponding carols 46, 47, 124, 164–184)

Who has believed our message and to whom has the arm of the Lord been revealed? He grew up before him like a tender shoot, and like a root out of dry ground. He had no beauty or majesty to attract us to him, nothing in his appearance that we should desire him. He was despised and rejected by men, a man of sorrows, and familiar with suffering. Like one from whom men hide their faces he was despised, and we esteemed him not.

Reader: This is the word of the Lord.
People: Thanks be to God.

4 The people have a King
(Matthew 2.1–12: corresponding carols 130–150)

After Jesus was born in Bethlehem in Judea, during the time of King Herod, Magi from the east came to Jerusalem and asked, 'Where is the one who has been born king of the Jews? We saw his star in the east and have come to worship him.' When King Herod heard this he was disturbed, and all Jerusalem with him. When he had called together all the people's chief priests and teachers of the law, he asked them where the Christ was to be born. 'In Bethlehem in Judea,' they replied, 'for this is what the prophet has written: "But you, Bethlehem, in the land of Judah, are by no means least among the rulers of Judah; for out of you will come a ruler who will be the shepherd of my people Israel."' Then Herod called the Magi secretly and found out from them the exact time the star had appeared. He sent them to Bethlehem and said, 'Go and make a careful search for the child. As soon as you find him, report to me, so that I too may go and worship him.' After they had heard the king, they went on their way, and the star they had seen in the east went ahead of them until it stopped over the place where the child was. When they saw the star, they were overjoyed. On coming to the house they saw the child with his mother Mary, and they bowed down and worshipped him. Then they opened their treasures and presented him with gifts of gold and of incense and of myrrh. And having been warned in a dream not to go back to Herod, they returned to their country by another route.

Reader: This is the word of the Lord.
People: Thanks be to God.

5 The people have a Counsellor
(Isaiah 9.6–7: corresponding carols 20 –22, 48, 73, 92–93, 126–127, 180)

For to us a child is born, to us a son is given, and the government will be on his shoulders. And he will be called Wonderful Counsellor, Mighty God, Everlasting Father, Prince of Peace. Of the increase of his government and peace there will be no end. He will reign on David's throne and over his kingdom, establishing and upholding it with justice and righteousness from that time on and for ever. The zeal of the Lord Almighty will accomplish this.

Reader: This is the word of the Lord.
People: Thanks be to God.

6 Some have accepted him
(John 1.1–5, 10–14: corresponding carols 52, 75, 81, 82, 123, 163, 167, 175, 176)

In the beginning was the Word, and the Word was with God, and the Word was God. He was with God in the beginning. Through him all things were made; without him nothing was made that has been made. In him was life, and that life was the light of men. The light shines in the darkness, but the darkness has not understood it. He was in the world, and though the world was made through him, the world did not recognise him. He came to that which was his own, but his own did not receive him. Yet to all who received him, to those who believed in his name, he gave the right to become children of God – children born not of natural descent, nor of human decision or a husband's will, but born of God. The Word became flesh and made his dwelling among us. We have seen his glory, the glory of the One and Only, who came from the Father, full of grace and truth.

Reader: This is the word of the Lord.
People: Thanks be to God.

CHRISTMAS READINGS
Third Set

THE PROMISE OF GOD – PROPHECY AND FULFILMENT
(Each Reading for two readers)

1 The sign of God's favour
(Isaiah 7.13, 14; Luke 1.26–35, 38: corresponding carols 24–27, 33, 75, 95, 121, 122)

A
Isaiah said, 'Hear now, you house of David! Is it not enough to try the patience of men? Will you try the patience of my God also? Therefore the Lord himself will give you a sign: The virgin will be with child and will give birth to a son, and will call him Immanuel.'

B
In the sixth month, God sent the angel Gabriel to Nazareth, a town in Galilee, to a virgin pledged to be married to a man named Joseph, a descendant of David. The virgin's name was Mary. The angel went to her and said, 'Greetings, you who are highly favoured! The Lord is with you.' Mary was greatly troubled at his words and wondered what kind of greeting this might be. But the angel said to her, 'Do not be afraid, Mary, you have found favour with God. You will be with child and give birth to a son, and you are to give him the name Jesus. He will be great and will be called the Son of the Most High. The Lord God will give him the throne of his father David, and he will reign over the house of Jacob for ever; his kingdom will never end.' 'How will this be,' Mary asked the angel, 'since I am a virgin?' The angel answered, 'The Holy Spirit will come upon you, and the power of the Most High will overshadow you. So the holy one to be born will be called the Son of God.' 'I am the Lord's servant,' Mary answered. 'May it be to me as you have said.' Then the angel left her.

Reader: This is the word of the Lord.
People: Thanks be to God.

2 The Son of David

(Isaiah 9.6–7; Luke 2.1, 3–7: corresponding carols 24, 73, 92–93, 126–127, 180)

A

To us a child is born, to us a son is given, and the government will be on his shoulders. And he will be called Wonderful Counsellor, Mighty God, Everlasting Father, Prince of Peace. Of the increase of his government and peace there will be no end. He will reign on David's throne and over his kingdom, establishing and upholding it with justice and righteousness from that time on and for ever.

B

In those days Caesar Augustus issued a decree that a census should be taken of the entire Roman world. And everyone went to his own town to register. So Joseph also went up from the town of Nazareth in Galilee to Judea, to Bethlehem the town of David, because he belonged to the house and line of David. He went there to register with Mary, who was pledged to be married to him and was expecting a child. While they were there, the time came for the baby to be born, and she gave birth to her firstborn, a son. She wrapped him in strips of cloth and placed him in a manger, because there was no room for them in the inn.

Reader: This is the word of the Lord.
People: Thanks be to God.

3 The light in the darkness

(Isaiah 9.2, 3, 4; Luke 2.8–14: corresponding carols 20–22; 77–100)

A

The people walking in darkness have seen a great light; on those living in the land of the shadow of death a light has dawned. You have enlarged the nation and increased their joy . . . For as in the day of Midian's defeat, you have shattered the yoke that burdens them, the bar across their shoulders, the rod of their oppressor.

B

And there were shepherds living out in the fields near by, keeping watch over their flocks at night. An angel of the Lord appeared to them, and the glory of the Lord shone around them, and they were terrified. But the angel said to them, 'Do not be afraid. I bring you good news of great joy that will be for all the people. Today in the town of David a Saviour has been born to you; he is Christ the Lord. This will be a sign to you: You will find a baby wrapped in strips of cloth and lying in a manger.' Suddenly a great company of the heavenly host appeared with the angel, praising God and saying, 'Glory to God in the highest, and on earth peace to men on whom his favour rests.'

Reader: This is the word of the Lord.
People: Thanks be to God.

4 The place of his birth

(Micah 5.2–5; Luke 2.15–20: corresponding carols 35, 40, 91, 134; 101–129)

A

'Bethlehem Ephrathah, though you are small among the clans of Judah, out of you will come for me one who will be ruler over Israel, whose origins are from of old, from ancient times.' Therefore Israel will be abandoned until the time when she who is in labour gives birth and the rest of his brothers return to join the Israelites. He will stand and shepherd his flock in the strength of the Lord, in the majesty of the name of the Lord his God. And they will live securely, for then his greatness will reach to the ends of the earth. And he will be their peace.

B

When the angels had left them and gone into heaven, the shepherds said to one another, 'Let's go to Bethlehem and see this thing that has happened, which the Lord has told us about.' So they hurried off and found Mary and Joseph, and the baby, who was lying in the manger. When they had seen him, they spread the word concerning what had been told them about this child, and all who heard it were amazed at what the shepherds said to them. But Mary treasured up all these things and pondered them in her heart. The shepherds returned, glorifying and praising God for all the things they had heard and seen, which were just as they had been told.

Reader: This is the word of the Lord.
People: Thanks be to God.

5 The star of his appearing
(Numbers 24.15–17; Matthew 2.1–2, 7–11: corresponding carols 117, 130–150)

A

The oracle of one whose eye sees clearly, the oracle of one who hears the words of God, who has knowledge from the Most High, who sees a vision from the Almighty, who falls prostrate, and whose eyes are opened: 'I see him, but not now; I behold him, but not near. A star will come out of Jacob; a sceptre will rise out of Israel.'

B

After Jesus was born in Bethlehem in Judea, during the time of King Herod, Magi from the east came to Jerusalem and asked, 'Where is the one who has been born king of the Jews? We saw his star in the east and have come to worship him.' Then Herod called the Magi secretly and found out from them the exact time the star had appeared. He sent them to Bethlehem and said, 'Go and make a careful search for the child. As soon as you find him, report to me, so that I too may go and worship him.' After they had heard the king, they went on their way, and the star they had seen in the east went ahead of them until it stopped over the place where the child was. When they saw the star, they were overjoyed. On coming to the house, they saw the child with his mother Mary, and they bowed down and worshipped him. Then they opened their treasures and presented him with gifts of gold and of incense and of myrrh.

Reader: This is the word of the Lord.
People: Thanks be to God.

6 The challenge of evil
(Jeremiah 31.15; Matthew 2.12–14, 16: corresponding carols 152–153, 151, 158–159)

A

This is what the Lord says: 'A voice is heard in Ramah, mourning and great weeping, Rachel weeping for her children and refusing to be comforted, because her children are no more.'

B

The Magi, having been warned in a dream not to go back to Herod, returned to their country by another route. When they had gone, an angel of the Lord appeared to Joseph in a dream. 'Get up,' he said, 'take the child and his mother and escape to Egypt. Stay there until I tell you, for Herod is going to search for the child to kill him.' So he got up, took the child and his mother during the night and left for Egypt. When Herod realised that he had been outwitted by the Magi, he was furious, and he gave orders to kill all the boys in Bethlehem and its vicinity who were two years old and under, in accordance with the time he had learned from the Magi.

Reader: This is the word of the Lord.
People: Thanks be to God.

7 The triumph of grace
(1 Peter 1.10, 11; Hebrews 1.1-3: corresponding carols 17, 124, 21–22, 91, 101–103, 179)

A

Concerning this salvation, the prophets, who spoke of the grace that was to come to you, searched intently and with the greatest care, trying to find out the time and circumstances to which the Spirit of Christ in them was pointing when he predicted the sufferings of Christ and the glories that would follow.

B

In the past God spoke to our forefathers through the prophets at many times and in various ways, but in these last days he has spoken to us by his Son, whom he appointed heir of all things, and through whom he made the universe. The Son is the radiance of God's glory and the exact representation of his being, sustaining all things by his powerful word. After he had provided purification for sins, he sat down at the right hand of the Majesty in heaven.

Reader: This is the word of the Lord.
People: Thanks be to God.

CHRISTMAS READINGS
Fourth Set

THE MEANING
OF CHRISTMAS –
WHO JESUS IS
(each reading for two readers)

1 The author of creation
(Genesis 1.1–5. Colossians 1.15–17: corresponding carols 3, 23, 72, 75)

A

In the beginning God created the heavens and the earth. Now the earth was formless and empty, darkness was over the surface of the deep, and the Spirit of God was hovering over the waters.

And God said, 'Let there be light,' and there was light. God saw that the light was good, and he separated the light from the darkness. God called the light 'day', and the darkness he called 'night'.

B

Christ is the image of the invisible God, the firstborn over all creation. For by him all things were created: things in heaven and on earth, visible and invisible, whether thrones or powers or rulers or authorities; all things were created by him and for him. He is before all things, and in him all things hold together.

Reader: This is the word of the Lord.
People: Thanks be to God.

2 The incarnation of love
(Luke 1.26–31, 34–35; Philippians 2.6–8: corresponding carols 25–27, 44, 171 –172, 173–176)

A

God sent the angel Gabriel to Nazareth, a town in Galilee, to a virgin pledged to be married to a man named Joseph, a descendant of David. The virgin's name was Mary. The angel went to her and said, 'Greetings, you who are highly favoured! The Lord is with you.' Mary was greatly troubled at his words and wondered what kind of greeting this might be. But the angel said to her, 'Do not be afraid, Mary, you have found favour with God. You will be with child

and give birth to a son, and you are to give him the name Jesus.' 'How will this be,' Mary asked the angel, 'since I am a virgin?' The angel answered, 'The Holy Spirit will come upon you, and the power of the Most High will overshadow you. So the holy one to be born will be called the Son of God.'

B

Christ Jesus . . . being in very nature God, did not consider equality with God something to be grasped, but made himself nothing, taking the very nature of a servant, being made in human likeness. And being found in appearance as a man, he humbled himself and became obedient to death – even death on a cross!

Reader: This is the word of the Lord.
People: Thanks be to God.

3 The promised one of Israel
(Luke 2.1–7; Galatians 4.4–7: corresponding carols 32–69)

A

In those days Caesar Augustus issued a decree that a census should be taken of the entire Roman world. And everyone went to his own town to register. So Joseph also went up from the town of Nazareth in Galilee to Judea, to Bethlehem the town of David, because he belonged to the house and line of David. He went there to register with Mary, who was pledged to be married to him and was expecting a child. While they were there, the time came for the baby to be born, and she gave birth to her firstborn, a son. She wrapped him in strips of cloth and placed him in a manger, because there was no room for them in the inn.

B

When the time had fully come, God sent his Son, born of a woman, born under law, to redeem those under law, that we might receive the full rights of sons. Because you are sons, God sent the Spirit of his Son into our hearts, the Spirit who calls out, 'Abba, Father.' So you are no longer a slave, but a son; and since you are a son, God has made you also an heir.

Reader: This is the word of the Lord.
People: Thanks be to God.

4 The light of God's glory
(Isaiah 9.2, 6–7; 2 Corinthians 4.4–6:
corresponding carols 20–22, 48, 59, 73,
80, 93, 126–127)

A
The people walking in darkness have
seen a great light; on those living in the
land of the shadow of death a light has
dawned. For to us a child is born, to us a
son is given, and the government will be
on his shoulders. And he will be called
Wonderful Counsellor, Mighty God,
Everlasting Father, Prince of Peace. Of
the increase of his government and peace
there will be no end. He will reign on
David's throne and over his kingdom,
establishing and upholding it with justice
and righteousness from that time on and
for ever. The zeal of the Lord Almighty
will accomplish this.

B
The god of this age has blinded the minds
of unbelievers, so that they cannot see
the light of the gospel of the glory of
Christ, who is the image of God. For we
do not preach ourselves, but Jesus Christ
as Lord, and ourselves as your servants
for Jesus' sake. For God, who said, 'Let
light shine out of darkness,' made his
light shine in our hearts to give us the
light of the knowledge of the glory of
God in the face of Christ.

Reader: This is the word of the Lord.
People: Thanks be to God.

5 The dawn of God's grace
(Luke 2.8–14; 1 John 4.7–9; Romans
13.11–12: corresponding carols 77–100;
164–169; 10, 118)

A
And there were shepherds living out in
the fields near Bethlehem, keeping watch
over their flocks at night. An angel of the
Lord appeared to them, and the glory of
the Lord shone around them, and they
were terrified. But the angel said to
them, 'Do not be afraid. I bring you good
news of great joy that will be for all the
people. Today in the town of David a
Saviour has been born to you; he is Christ
the Lord. This will be a sign to you: You
will find a baby wrapped in strips of cloth
and lying in a manger.' Suddenly a great
company of the heavenly host appeared

with the angel, praising God and saying,
'Glory to God in the highest, and on earth
peace to men on whom his favour rests.'

B
Dear friends, let us love one another, for
love comes from God. Everyone who
loves has been born of God and knows
God. Whoever does not love does not
know God, because God is love. This is
how God showed his love among us: He
sent his one and only Son into the world
that we might live through him.

A
The hour has come for you to wake up
from your slumber, because our salvation is nearer now than when we first
believed. The night is nearly over; the
day is almost here. So let us put aside the
deeds of darkness and put on the armour
of light.

Reader: This is the word of the Lord.
People: Thanks be to God.

6 The expression of God's Being
(Luke 2.15–18, 20; Hebrews 1.1–3: corresponding carols 101–129, 158–159; 17,
20–23, 100–103)

A
When the angels had left them and gone
into heaven, the shepherds said to one
another, 'Let's go to Bethlehem and see
this thing that has happened, which the
Lord has told us about.' So they hurried
off and found Mary and Joseph, and the
baby, who was lying in the manger.
When they had seen him, they spread the
word concerning what had been told
them about this child, and all who heard
it were amazed at what the shepherds
said to them. The shepherds returned,
glorifying and praising God for all the
things they had heard and seen, which
were just as they had been told.

B
In the past God spoke to our forefathers
through the prophets at many times and
in various ways, but in these last days he
has spoken to us by his Son, whom he
appointed heir of all things, and through
whom he made the universe. The Son is
the radiance of God's glory and the exact
representation of his being, sustaining all
things by his powerful word. After he had

provided purification for sins, he sat down at the right hand of the Majesty in heaven.

Reader: This is the word of the Lord.
People: Thanks be to God.

7 The Word of the Father
(John 1.1–5; John 1.10–13; John 1.14: corresponding carols 19, 45–47, 52, 75, 81, 86, 118, 163)

A

In the beginning was the Word, and the Word was with God, and the Word was God. He was with God in the beginning. Through him all things were made; without him nothing was made that has been made. In him was life, and that life was the light of men. The light shines in the darkness, but the darkness has not understood it.

B

He was in the world, and though the world was made through him, the world did not recognise him. He came to that which was his own, but his own did not receive him. Yet to all who received him, to those who believed in his name, he gave the right to become children of God – children born not of natural descent, nor of human decision or a husband's will, but born of God.

A

The Word became flesh and made his dwelling among us. We have seen his glory, the glory of the One and Only, who came from the Father, full of grace and truth.

Reader: This is the word of the Lord.
People: Thanks be to God.

CHRISTMAS READINGS
Fifth Set

THE CHRISTMAS STORY

1 The prophets promise the saviour
(Numbers 24.16, 17; Isaiah 7.14; Jeremiah 23.5, 6; Micah 5.2, 4; Isaiah 9.6: corresponding carols 1, 20–22, 39–40, 91, 95, 134)

Numbers
The oracle of one who hears the words of God, who has knowledge from the Most High: I see him, but not now; I behold him, but not near. A star will come out of Jacob; a sceptre will rise out of Israel.

Isaiah
The Lord himself will give you a sign: The virgin will be with child and will give birth to a son, and will call him Immanuel.

Jeremiah
'The days are coming,' declares the Lord, 'when I will raise up to David a righteous Branch, a King who will reign wisely and do what is just and right in the land. This is the name by which he will be called: The Lord Our Righteousness.'

Micah
Bethlehem Ephrathah, though you are small among the clans of Judah, out of you will come for me one who will be ruler over Israel, whose origins are from of old, from ancient times. He will stand and shepherd his flock in the strength of the Lord, in the majesty of the name of the Lord his God.

Isaiah
To us a child is born, to us a son is given, and the government will be on his shoulders. And he will be called Wonderful Counsellor, Mighty God, Everlasting Father, Prince of Peace.

Reader: This is the word of the Lord.
People: Thanks be to God.

2 Mary hears the news
(from Luke 1.26–38: corresponding carols 25–29)

Narrator
In the sixth month, God sent the angel Gabriel to Nazareth, a town in Galilee, to a virgin pledged to be married to a man named Joseph, a descendant of David. The virgin's name was Mary. The angel went to her and said:

Angel
Greetings, you who are highly favoured! The Lord is with you.

Narrator
Mary was greatly troubled at his words and wondered what kind of greeting this might be. But the angel said to her:

Angel
Do not be afraid, Mary, you have found favour with God. You will be with child and give birth to a son, and you are to give him the name Jesus. He will be great and will be called the Son of the Most High. The Lord God will give him the throne of his father David, and he will reign over the house of Jacob for ever; his kingdom will never end.

Narrator
Mary asked the angel:

Mary
How will this be, since I am a virgin?

Angel
The Holy Spirit will come upon you, and the power of the Most High will over-shadow you. So the holy one to be born will be called the Son of God.

Narrator
Mary answered:

Mary
I am the Lord's servant. May it be to me as you have said.

Narrator
Then the angel left her.

Reader: This is the word of the Lord.
People: Thanks be to God.

3 Joseph learns the truth
(from Matthew 1.18–25: corresponding carols 30–31; 43–56)

Narrator
This is how the birth of Jesus Christ came about: His mother Mary was pledged to be married to Joseph, but before they came together, she was found to be with child through the Holy Spirit. Because Joseph her husband was a righteous man and did not want to expose her to public disgrace, he had in mind to divorce her quietly. But after he had considered this, an angel of the Lord appeared to him in a dream and said:

Angel
Joseph son of David, do not be afraid to take Mary home as your wife, because what is conceived in her is from the Holy Spirit. She will give birth to a son, and you are to give him the name Jesus, because he will save his people from their sins.

Narrator
All this took place to fulfil what the Lord had said through the prophet:

Prophet
The virgin will be with child and will give birth to a son, and they will call him Immanuel – God with us.

Narrator
When Joseph woke up, he did what the angel of the Lord had commanded him and took Mary home as his wife. But he had no union with her until she gave birth to a son. And he gave him the name Jesus.

Reader: This is the word of the Lord.
People: Thanks be to God.

4 The angels announce the birth
(from Luke 2.8–14: corresponding carols 77–100)

Narrator:
There were shepherds living out in the fields near Bethlehem, keeping watch over their flocks at night. An angel of the Lord appeared to them, and the glory of the Lord shone around them, and they were terrified. But the angel said to them:

Angel
Do not be afraid. I bring you good news of great joy that will be for all the people. Today in the town of David a Saviour has been born to you; he is Christ the Lord. This will be a sign to you: You will find a baby wrapped in strips of cloth and lying in a manger.

Narrator
Suddenly a great company of the heavenly host appeared with the angel, praising God and saying:

Chorus
Glory to God in the highest, and on

earth peace to men on whom his favour rests.

Reader: This is the word of the Lord.
People: Thanks be to God.

5 The shepherds find the baby
(from Luke 2.15–20: corresponding carols 101–129)

Narrator
When the angels had left them and gone into heaven, the shepherds said to one another:

Shepherds
Let's go to Bethlehem and see this thing that has happened, which the Lord has told us about.

Narrator
So they hurried off and found Mary and Joseph, and the baby, who was lying in the manger. When they had seen him, they spread the word concerning what had been told them about this child, and all who heard it were amazed at what the shepherds said to them. But Mary treasured up all these things and pondered them in her heart. The shepherds returned, glorifying and praising God for all the things they had heard and seen, which were just as they had been told.

Reader: This is the word of the Lord.
People: Thanks be to God.

6 The wise men follow the star
(from Matthew 2.1–11: corresponding carols 130–141)

Narrator
After Jesus was born in Bethlehem in Judea, during the time of King Herod, Magi from the east came to Jerusalem and asked:

Magi
Where is the one who has been born king of the Jews? We saw his star in the east and have come to worship him.

Narrator
When King Herod heard this he was disturbed, and all Jerusalem with him. When he had called together all the people's chief priests and teachers of the law, he asked them:

Herod
Where will the Christ be born?

Narrator
They replied:

Teachers
In Bethlehem in Judea, for this is what the prophet has written: 'Bethlehem in the land of Judah, out of you will come a ruler who will be the shepherd of my people Israel.'

Narrator
Then Herod called the Magi secretly and found out from them the exact time the star had appeared. He sent them to Bethlehem and said:

Herod
Go and make a careful search for the child. As soon as you find him, report to me, so that I too may go and worship him.

Narrator
After they had heard the king, they went on their way, and the star they had seen in the east went ahead of them until it stopped over the place where the child was. When they saw the star, they were overjoyed. On coming to the house, they saw the child with his mother Mary, and they bowed down and worshipped him. Then they opened their treasures and presented him with gifts of gold and of incense and of myrrh.

Reader: This is the word of the Lord.
People: Thanks be to God.

7 The child escapes the sword
(from Matthew 2.13–18: corresponding carols 142–153. This reading may be omitted at Christmas if desired.)

Narrator
When the Magi had gone, an angel of the Lord appeared to Joseph in a dream. He said:

Angel
Get up, take the child and his mother and escape to Egypt. Stay there until I tell

you, for Herod is going to search for the child to kill him.

Narrator
So Joseph got up, took the child and his mother during the night and left for Egypt, where he stayed until the death of Herod. And so was fulfilled what the Lord had said through the prophet:

Prophet
Out of Egypt I called my son.

Narrator
When Herod realised that he had been outwitted by the Magi, he was furious, and he gave orders to kill all the boys in Bethlehem and its vicinity who were two years old and under, in accordance with the time he had learned from the Magi. Then what was said through the prophet Jeremiah was fulfilled:

Prophet
A voice is heard in Ramah, weeping and great mourning, Rachel weeping for her children and refusing to be comforted, because they are no more.

Reader: This is the word of the Lord.
People: Thanks be to God.

8 **Simeon recognises the messiah**
(from Luke 2.25–32: corresponding carols 154–159. This reading may be omitted at Christmas if desired.)

Narrator
Now there was a man in Jerusalem called Simeon, who was righteous and devout. He was waiting for the consolation of Israel, and the Holy Spirit was upon him. It had been revealed to him by the Holy Spirit that he would not die before he had seen the Lord's Christ. Moved by the Spirit, he went into the temple courts. When the parents brought in the child Jesus to do for him what the custom of the Law required, Simeon took him in his arms and praised God, saying:

Simeon
Sovereign Lord, as you have promised, you now dismiss your servant in peace. For my eyes have seen your salvation, which you have prepared in the sight of all people, a light for revelation to the Gentiles and for glory to your people Israel.

Narrator
The child's father and mother marvelled at what was said about him. Then Simeon blessed them and said to Mary, his mother:

Simeon
This child is destined to cause the falling and rising of many in Israel, and to be a sign that will be spoken against, so that the thoughts of many hearts will be revealed. And a sword will pierce your own soul too.

Reader: This is the word of the Lord.
People: Thanks be to God.

9 **The apostles explain the meaning**
(John 1.1, 3, 14; Colossians 1.15, 17; Hebrews 1.1, 2, 3; 2 Corinthians 4.6, 8.9; Philippians 2.6; John 1.11–12: corresponding carols 19, 21–23, 45, 55, 72, 75, 81, 82, 91, 101, 163, 167, 171–176)

John
In the beginning was the Word, and the Word was with God, and the Word was God. Through him all things were made. The Word became flesh and made his dwelling among us. We have seen his glory, the glory of the One and Only, who came from the Father, full of grace and truth.

Colossians
Christ is the image of the invisible God, the firstborn over all creation. He is before all things, and in him all things hold together.

Hebrews
In the past God spoke to our forefathers through the prophets, but in these last days he has spoken to us by his Son, who is the radiance of his glory and the exact representation of his being.

2 Corinthians
God, who said, 'Let light shine out of darkness,' made his light shine in our hearts to give us the light of the knowledge of the glory of God in the face of Christ. You know the grace of our Lord Jesus Christ, that though he was rich, yet for your sakes he became poor, so that you through his poverty might become rich.

Philippians
Christ Jesus, being in very nature God, did not consider equality with God something to be grasped, but made himself nothing, taking the very nature of a servant, being made in human likeness.

John
He came to that which was his own, but his own did not receive him. Yet to all who received him, to those who believed in his name, he gave the right to become children of God.

Reader: This is the word of the Lord.
People: Thanks be to God.

CHRISTMAS READINGS
Sixth Set

THE NINE LESSONS
(Traditional Readings)

1 God declares his judgement
(Genesis 3.8–15: corresponding carol 97)

Then the man and his wife heard the sound of the Lord God as he was walking in the garden in the cool of the day, and they hid from the Lord God among the trees of the garden. But the Lord God called to the man, 'Where are you?' He answered, 'I heard you in the garden, and I was afraid because I was naked; so I hid.' And God said, 'Who told you that you were naked? Have you eaten from the tree from which I commanded you not to eat?' The man said, 'The woman you put here with me – she gave me some fruit from the tree, and I ate it.' Then the Lord God said to the woman, 'What is this you have done?' The woman said, 'The serpent deceived me, and I ate.' So the Lord God said to the serpent, 'Because you have done this, cursed are you above all the livestock and all the wild animals! You will crawl on your belly and you will eat dust all the days of your life. And I will put enmity between you and the woman, and between your offspring and hers; he will crush your head, and you will strike his heel.'

Reader: This is the word of the Lord.
People: Thanks be to God.

2 Isaiah announces the coming king
(Isaiah 9.2, 6–7: corresponding carols 20–22, 93)

The people walking in darkness have seen a great light; on those living in the land of the shadow of death a light has dawned. For to us a child is born, to us a son is given, and the government will be on his shoulders. And he will be called Wonderful Counsellor, Mighty God, Everlasting Father, Prince of Peace. Of the increase of his government and peace there will be no end. He will reign on David's throne and over his kingdom, establishing and upholding it with justice and righteousness from that time on and for ever. The zeal of the Lord Almighty will accomplish this.

Reader: This is the word of the Lord.
People: Thanks be to God.

3 EITHER God promises a ruler from Bethlehem
(Micah 5.2–5: corresponding carols 39–40, 91, 134)

'Bethlehem Ephrathah, though you are small among the clans of Judah, out of you will come for me one who will be ruler over Israel, whose origins are from of old, from ancient times.' Therefore Israel will be abandoned until the time when she who is in labour gives birth and the rest of his brothers return to join the Israelites. He will stand and shepherd his flock in the strength of the Lord, in the majesty of the name of the Lord his God. And they will live securely, for then his greatness will reach to the ends of the earth. And he will be their peace.

Reader: This is the word of the Lord.
People: Thanks be to God.

OR God promises a ruler from David's family
(Isaiah 11.1–5: corresponding carols 1, 24, 161–162)

A shoot will come up from the stump of Jesse; from his roots a Branch will bear fruit. The Spirit of the Lord will rest on him – the Spirit of wisdom and of understanding, the Spirit of counsel and of power, the Spirit of knowledge and of the fear of the Lord – and he will delight in the fear of the Lord. He will not judge by what he sees with his eyes, or decide by what he hears with his ears; but with righteousness he will judge the needy, with justice he will give decisions for the poor of the earth. He will strike the earth with the rod of his mouth; with the breath of his lips he will slay the wicked. Righteousness will be his belt and faithfulness the sash round his waist.

Reader: This is the word of the Lord.
People: Thanks be to God.

4 The angel comes to Mary
(Luke 1.26–33, 38: corresponding carols 25–29)

In the sixth month, God sent the angel Gabriel to Nazareth, a town in Galilee, to a virgin pledged to be married to a man named Joseph, a descendant of David. The virgin's name was Mary. The angel went to her and said, 'Greetings, you who are highly favoured! The Lord is with you.' Mary was greatly troubled at his words and wondered what kind of greeting this might be. But the angel said to her, 'Do not be afraid, Mary, you have found favour with God. You will be with child and give birth to a son, and you are to give him the name Jesus. He will be great and will be called the Son of the Most High. The Lord God will give him the throne of his father David, and he will reign over the house of Jacob for ever; his kingdom will never end.' 'I am the Lord's servant,' Mary answered. 'May it be to me as you have said.' Then the angel left her.

Reader: This is the word of the Lord.
People: Thanks be to God.

5 God's purpose is explained to Joseph
(Matthew 1.18–25a: corresponding carols 30–31, 33, 75, 84, 95, 121)

This is how the birth of Jesus Christ came about: His mother Mary was pledged to be married to Joseph, but before they came together, she was found to be with child through the Holy Spirit. Because Joseph her husband was a righteous man and did not want to expose her to public disgrace, he had in mind to divorce her quietly. But after he had considered this, an angel of the Lord appeared to him in a dream and said, 'Joseph son of David, do not be afraid to take Mary home as your wife, because what is conceived in her is from the Holy Spirit. She will give birth to a son, and you are to give him the name Jesus, because he will save his people from their sins.' All this took place to fulfil what the Lord had said through the prophet: 'The virgin will be with child and will give birth to a son, and they will call him Immanuel' – which means, 'God with us'. When Joseph woke up, he did what the angel of the Lord had commanded him and took Mary home as his wife. But he had no union with her until she gave birth to a son.

Reader: This is the word of the Lord.
People: Thanks be to God.

6 Jesus is born
(Luke 2.1–7: corresponding carols 32–76)

In those days Caesar Augustus issued a decree that a census should be taken of the entire Roman world. This was the first census that took place while Quirinius was governor of Syria. And everyone went to his own town to register. So Joseph also went up from the town of Nazareth in Galilee to Judea, to Bethlehem the town of David, because he belonged to the house and line of David. He went there to register with Mary, who was pledged to be married to him and was expecting a child. While they were there, the time came for the baby to be born, and she gave birth to her firstborn, a son. She wrapped him in strips of cloth and placed him in a manger, because there was no room for them in the inn.

Reader: This is the word of the Lord.
People: Thanks be to God.

7 The shepherds go to the stable
(Luke 2.8–16: corresponding carols 77 –129)

There were shepherds living out in the fields near Bethlehem, keeping watch over their flocks at night. An angel of the

Lord appeared to them, and the glory of the Lord shone around them, and they were terrified. But the angel said to them, 'Do not be afraid. I bring you good news of great joy that will be for all the people. Today in the town of David a Saviour has been born to you; he is Christ the Lord. This will be a sign to you: You will find a baby wrapped in strips of cloth and lying in a manger.' Suddenly a great company of the heavenly host appeared with the angel, praising God and saying, 'Glory to God in the highest, and on earth peace to men on whom his favour rests.' When the angels had left them and gone into heaven, the shepherds said to one another, 'Let's go to Bethlehem and see this thing that has happened, which the Lord has told us about.' So they hurried off and found Mary and Joseph, and the baby, who was lying in the manger.

Reader: This is the word of the Lord.
People: Thanks be to God.

8 Travellers come from the east
(Matthew 2.1–2, 7–11: corresponding carols 130–150)

After Jesus was born in Bethlehem in Judea, during the time of King Herod, Magi from the east came to Jerusalem and asked, 'Where is the one who has been born king of the Jews? We saw his star in the east and have come to worship him.' Then Herod called the Magi secretly and found out from them the exact time the star had appeared. He sent them to Bethlehem and said, 'Go and make a careful search for the child. As soon as you find him, report to me, so that I too may go and worship him.' After they had heard the king, they went on their way, and the star they had seen in the east went ahead of them until it stopped over the place where the child was. When they saw the star, they were overjoyed. On coming to the house, they saw the child with his mother Mary, and they bowed down and worshipped him. Then they opened their treasures and presented him with gifts of gold and of incense and of myrrh.

Reader: This is the word of the Lord.
People: Thanks be to God.

9 The Word becomes flesh
(John 1.1–14: corresponding carols 19, 45, 52, 75, 81–82, 100, 162–163, 167)

In the beginning was the Word, and the Word was with God, and the Word was God. He was with God in the beginning. Through him all things were made; without him nothing was made that has been made. In him was life, and that life was the light of men. The light shines in the darkness, but the darkness has not understood it. There came a man who was sent from God; his name was John. He came as a witness to testify concerning that light, so that through him all men might believe. He himself was not the light; he came only as a witness to the light. The true light that gives light to every man was coming into the world. He was in the world, and though the world was made through him, the world did not recognise him. He came to that which was his own, but his own did not receive him. Yet to all who received him, to those who believed in his name, he gave the right to become children of God – children born not of natural descent, nor of human decision or a husband's will, but born of God. The Word became flesh and made his dwelling among us. We have seen his glory, the glory of the One and Only, who came from the Father, full of grace and truth.

Reader: This is the word of the Lord.
People: Thanks be to God.

EPIPHANY READINGS

PROCLAIMING THE SAVIOUR

1 The light of the world
(Isaiah 60.1–5a: corresponding carol 140)

'Arise, shine, for your light has come, and the glory of the Lord rises upon you. See, darkness covers the earth and thick darkness is over the peoples, but the Lord rises upon you and his glory appears over you. Nations will come to your light, and kings to the brightness of your dawn.

Lift up your eyes and look about you: All assemble and come to you; your sons come from afar, and your daughters are carried on the arm. Then you will look and be radiant, your heart will throb and swell with joy.'

Reader: This is the word of the Lord.
People: Thanks be to God.

2 The king of the Jews
(Matthew 2.1–2, 7–12: corresponding carols 130–150)

After Jesus was born in Bethlehem in Judea, during the time of King Herod, Magi from the east came to Jerusalem and asked, 'Where is the one who has been born king of the Jews? We saw his star in the east and have come to worship him.' Then Herod called the Magi secretly and found out from them the exact time the star had appeared. He sent them to Bethlehem and said, 'Go and make a careful search for the child. As soon as you find him, report to me, so that I too may go and worship him.' After they had heard the king, they went on their way, and the star they had seen in the east went ahead of them until it stopped over the place where the child was. When they saw the star, they were overjoyed. On coming to the house, they saw the child with his mother Mary, and they bowed down and worshipped him. Then they opened their treasures and presented him with gifts of gold and of incense and of myrrh. And having been warned in a dream not to go back to Herod, they returned to their country by another route.

Reader: This is the word of the Lord.
People: Thanks be to God.

3 The child of destiny
(Matthew 2.13–18: corresponding carols 152–153)

When they had gone, an angel of the Lord appeared to Joseph in a dream. 'Get up,' he said, 'take the child and his mother and escape to Egypt. Stay there until I tell you, for Herod is going to search for the child to kill him.' So he got up, took the child and his mother during the night and left for Egypt, where he stayed until the death of Herod. And so was fulfilled what the Lord had said

through the prophet, 'Out of Egypt I called my son.' When Herod realised that he had been outwitted by the Magi, he was furious, and he gave orders to kill all the boys in Bethlehem and its vicinity who were two years old and under, in accordance with the time he had learned from the Magi. Then what was said through the prophet Jeremiah was fulfilled: 'A voice is heard in Ramah, weeping and great mourning, Rachel weeping for her children and refusing to be comforted, because they are no more.'

Reader: This is the word of the Lord.
People: Thanks be to God.

4 The prophet of Nazareth
(Matthew 2.19–23: corresponding carol 151)

After Herod died, an angel of the Lord appeared in a dream to Joseph in Egypt and said, 'Get up, take the child and his mother and go to the land of Israel, for those who were trying to take the child's life are dead.' So he got up, took the child and his mother and went to the land of Israel. But when he heard that Archelaus was reigning in Judea in place of his father Herod, he was afraid to go there. Having been warned in a dream, he withdrew to the district of Galilee, and he went and lived in a town called Nazareth. So was fulfilled what was said through the prophets: 'He will be called a Nazarene.'

Reader: This is the word of the Lord.
People: Thanks be to God.

5 The consolation of Israel
(Luke 2.22–28 or 22–32: corresponding carols 154–157)

When the time of their purification according to the Law of Moses had been completed, Joseph and Mary took Jesus to Jerusalem to present him to the Lord (as it is written in the Law of the Lord, 'Every firstborn male is to be consecrated to the Lord'), and to offer a sacrifice in keeping with what is said in the Law of the Lord: 'a pair of doves or two young pigeons'. Now there was a man in Jerusalem called Simeon, who was righteous and devout. He was waiting for the consolation of Israel, and the Holy Spirit was upon him. It had been revealed to him by the Holy Spirit that he would not die before he had seen the Lord's Christ. Moved by the Spirit, he went into the temple courts. When the parents brought in the child Jesus to do for him what the custom of the Law required, Simeon took him in his arms and praised God.*

Reader: This is the word of the Lord.
People: Thanks be to God.

(*Here follows *The Song of Simeon/Nunc dimittis*)

6 The infant of Mary
(Luke 2.33–40: corresponding carols 158 –159)

The child's father and mother marvelled at what was said about him. Then Simeon blessed them and said to Mary, his mother: 'This child is destined to cause the falling and rising of many in Israel, and to be a sign that will be spoken against, so that the thoughts of many hearts will be revealed. And a sword will pierce your own soul too.'

There was also a prophetess, Anna, the daughter of Phanuel, of the tribe of Asher. She was very old; she had lived with her husband seven years after her marriage, and then was a widow until she was eighty-four. She never left the temple but worshipped night and day, fasting and praying. Coming up to them at that very moment, she gave thanks to God and spoke about the child to all who were looking forward to the redemption of Jerusalem. When Joseph and Mary had done everything required by the Law of the Lord, they returned to Galilee to their own town of Nazareth. And the child grew and became strong; he was filled with wisdom, and the grace of God was upon him.

Reader: This is the word of the Lord.
People: Thanks be to God.

7 EITHER The Son of God
(Matthew 3.13–17: corresponding carols 160–162)

Then Jesus came from Galilee to the Jordan to be baptised by John. But John tried to deter him, saying, 'I need to be baptised by you, and do you come to me?' Jesus replied, 'Let it be so now; it is proper for us to do this to fulfil all righteousness.' Then John consented. As soon as Jesus was baptised, he went up out of the water. At that moment heaven was opened, and he saw the Spirit of God descending like a dove and lighting on him. And a voice from heaven said, 'This is my Son, whom I love; with him I am well pleased.'

Reader: This is the word of the Lord.
People: Thanks be to God.

OR The servant of the Lord
(Isaiah 42.1–7: corresponding carols 14, 17, 126–127, 154–157)

'Here is my servant, whom I uphold, my chosen one in whom I delight; I will put my Spirit on him and he will bring justice to the nations. He will not shout or cry out, or raise his voice in the streets. A bruised reed he will not break, and a smouldering wick he will not snuff out. In faithfulness he will bring forth justice; he will not falter or be discouraged till he establishes justice on earth. In his law the islands will put their hope.'

This is what God the Lord says – he who created the heavens and stretched them out, who spread out the earth and all that comes out of it, who gives breath to its people, and life to those who walk on it: 'I, the Lord, have called you in righteousness; I will take hold of your hand. I will keep you and will make you to be a covenant for the people and a light for the Gentiles, to open eyes that are blind, to free captives from prison and to release from the dungeon those who sit in darkness.'

Reader: This is the word of the Lord.
People: Thanks be to God.

8 EITHER The hope of the world
(Romans 15.4–9, 11, 12–13: corresponding carols 8, 17, 19, 24, 91–97, 161–162)

Everything that was written in the past was written to teach us, so that through endurance and the encouragement of the Scriptures we might have hope. May the God who gives endurance and encouragement give you a spirit of unity among yourselves as you follow Christ Jesus, so that with one heart and mouth you may glorify the God and Father of our Lord Jesus Christ. Accept one another, then, just as Christ accepted you, in order to bring praise to God. For I tell you that Christ has become a servant of the Jews on behalf of God's truth, to confirm the promises made to the patriarchs so that the Gentiles may glorify God for his mercy, as it is written . . . 'Praise the Lord, all you Gentiles, and sing praises to him, all you peoples.' 'The Root of Jesse will spring up, one who will arise to rule over the nations; the Gentiles will hope in him.' May the God of hope fill you with all joy and peace as you trust in him, so that you may overflow with hope by the power of the Holy Spirit.

Reader: This is the word of the Lord.
People: Thanks be to God.

OR **The word of truth**
(Romans 10.8–17: corresponding carols 8, 16, 17, 19, 91, 93)

'The word is near you; it is in your mouth and in your heart,' that is, the word of faith we are proclaiming: That if you confess with your mouth, 'Jesus is Lord,' and believe in your heart that God raised him from the dead, you will be saved. For it is with your heart that you believe and are justified, and it is with your mouth that you confess and are saved. As the Scripture says, 'Anyone who trusts in him will never be put to shame.'

For there is no difference between Jew and Gentile – the same Lord is Lord of all and richly blesses all who call on him, for, 'Everyone who calls on the name of the Lord will be saved.' How, then, can they call on the one they have not believed in? And how can they believe in the one of whom they have not heard? And how can they hear without someone preaching to them? And how can they preach unless they are sent? As it is written, 'How beautiful are the feet of those who bring good news!' But not all the Israelites accepted the good news. For Isaiah says, 'Lord, who has believed our message?' Consequently, faith comes from hearing the message, and the message is heard through the word of Christ.

Reader: This is the word of the Lord.
People: Thanks be to God.

ACKNOWLEDGEMENTS

To every author, composer and arranger who took part in the making of CAROLS FOR TODAY, we express our appreciation. Several were drawn to make textual and musical adjustments to their own works specially for us, and to them in particular we are humbly grateful.

We owe our thanks not only to those who contributed words and music for this book, but to all who inspired its character: in particular to the rest of the Jubilate team under Bishop Michael Baughen. That most prolific of modern carol writers Bishop Timothy Dudley-Smith, our colleague of earlier days, gave a head-start to the task, as did the compilers of the previous standard books. We thank our publishers – Hodder & Stoughton – for having faith in us and commissioning this volume before they knew that Jubilate's 'Hymns for Today's Church' was going to have the wide success it now enjoys.

The vision for a colloquial carol book has its origins some twenty-five years ago when, as verbal and musical novices, we all sought to bring to the young people within our pastoral care the Good News of Christ in a language and idiom they might understand and to which they could respond. Youth passed into adulthood, and the vision widened; but the gap between creed and credence was ever there to be bridged. For the encouragement to build bridges in verse and song we thank all those who over the years have used our material – and have come back for more.

Associated with this particular volume are the experts who assisted with, or confirmed, our translation of foreign and classical carol texts: Ester Jensen (Danish), Annemarie Von Rad and Gisela Whittingham (German), Deborah Stokes (French), and Ursula Baker (Latin).

Our thanks for careful criticism of music go to John Barnard, and of text to Christopher Idle and Timothy Dudley-Smith. For the massive amount of copyright processing, painstaking checking, text adjustment and computer programming, we thank Bunty Grundy and her team: Sylvia Bleasdale, Ann Darlington and Sally Solomon, as well as Norman and Joan Gutteridge and Paul Wigmore.

To you, the peruser and user of CAROLS FOR TODAY, we say 'thank you' for considering, and applying your musical skills to this offering of our hearts and minds for the glory of God.

MICHAEL PERRY (EDITOR)
DAVID ILIFF (MUSIC EDITOR)

LEGAL INFORMATION

Carols
Those seeking to reprint works in this book which are the property of Jubilate Hymns or associated authors (indicated by an obelisk, †), including items by Word & Music, may write to The Copyright Secretary, Jubilate Hymns Ltd., 61 Chessel Avenue, Southampton SO2 4DY. Addresses of other copyright holders can also be supplied.

A number of Church music publishers have uniform concessions and rates. Details are available from the Copyright Secretary, Jubilate Hymns Ltd.

Most of these publishers also combine to offer a licensing scheme for limited term reproduction. Where this is felt to be an advantage, application should be made to the Christian Music Publishers' Association at PO Box 75, Eastbourne BN23 6NW, or at Northbridge Road, Berkhamsted, Herts HP4 1EH. Hymns copyrighted Stainer and Bell may not be reprinted or photocopied under any blanket licensing scheme, but should be cleared individually with Stainer & Bell. Items copyrighted Boosey & Hawkes and OUP are used with their kind permission.

Prayers
Individual prayers in this book, though not all subject to copyright control, should not be reprinted without obtaining, where possible, the author's permission.

Material from *The Alternative Service Book 1980* is the copyright of the Central Board of Finance of the Church of England, and is used by permission.

The text of the Apostles' Creed, as printed in CAROLS FOR TODAY, is copyright© 1970, 1971, 1975 International Consultation on English Texts (ICET). The Lord's Prayer in its modern form is adapted from the ICET version.

The Christmas 'Thanksgiving' prayer comes from the book *When you pray with 7's–10's* and is used by permission.

Material from *Worship Now* is used by permission of the St Andrew Press, Church of Scotland.

Material from *The Alternative Prayer Book* is printed with the permission of the General Synod of the Church of Ireland.

Readings and Quotations
Text from the New International Version (copyright © 1973, 1978, 1984 by International Bible Society) is used with the permission of Hodder and Stoughton, 47 Bedford Square, London WC1B 3DP. The form of the dramatised readings (Christmas, Fifth set: 'The Christmas Story') is copyright © Word & Music†.

Recording and Broadcasting
Jubilate Hymns with associated authors and composers (indicated by an obelisk, †), and Word & Music are members of the Mechanical Copyright Protection, and Performing Right Societies.

CAROL SHEETS

Inexpensive words sheets containing the non-specialist items in CAROLS FOR TODAY are available in quantity from Jubilate Hymns Ltd at 61 Chessel Avenue, Southampton SO2 4DY.

BIBLE REFERENCES

Genesis
2.15   God to Adam came in Eden – 97
3.16   Joy to the world! The Lord has come – 18

Numbers
24.16   A child this day is born – 117
24.17   O come, O come, Emmanuel – 1

1 Samuel
15.29   Come, O long-expected Jesus – 2
15.29   Faithful vigil ended – 154

Job
4.19   Behold, the great Creator makes – 175, 176

Psalm
2.9   Your kingdom come – 4
8.4   I wonder as I wander – 169
24.7   Lift up your heads, you mighty gates – 6
44.26   Your kingdom come – 4
51.17   Brightest and best – 140
85.   The Lord will come and not be slow – 7
86.   The Lord will come and not be slow – 7
96.8,9   O worship the Lord in the beauty of holiness – 150
98.7   A great and mighty wonder – 95

Song of Songs
5.2   Wake, O wake, and sleep no longer – 10

Isaiah
7.14   A great and mighty wonder – 95
7.14   A virgin most holy – 33
7.14   Christmas for God's holy people – 122
7.14   God of God, the uncreated – 75
7.14   Had he not loved us – 166
7.14   Hark! the herald angels sing – 84
7.14   O come, all ye faithful – 102, 103
7.14   O come, O come, Emmanuel – 1
7.14   The darkness turns to dawn – 21, 22
7.14   The virgin Mary had a baby boy – 121
9.2   The darkness turns to dawn – 21, 22
9.2   The people who in darkness walked – 20
9.6   A child is born in Bethlehem – 126, 127
9.6   It came upon the midnight clear – 92
9.6   Mary had a baby – sweet lamb – 48

9.6	O Babe divine, to you we sing – 180
9.6	O Prince of peace – 93
9.6	Sing, oh sing, this happy morn – 73
9.6	The darkness turns to dawn – 21, 22
11.1	A tender shoot has started – 24
11.1	O come, O come, Emmanuel – 1
11.1	Songs of thankfulness and praise – 161, 162
22.22	O come, O come, Emmanuel – 1
29.5	Child of the stable's secret birth – 46, 47
35.	Joy to the world! The Lord has come – 18
40.3	On Jordan's bank the Baptist's cry – 160
40.6	Take God's good news to saddened hearts – 8
41.2	People, look east – 13
45.2	Hark the glad sound – 14
45.23	Angels from the realms of glory – 86
51.17	Wake, O wake, and sleep no longer – 10
52.8	We hail the approaching God – 16
59.20	O come, our world's Redeemer, come – 5
60.6	Brightest and best – 140
61.1	A child is born in Bethlehem – 126, 127
61.1,10	Hark the glad sound – 14
62.10	Jesus the saviour comes – 15

Jeremiah

23.5	A child is born in Bethlehem – 126, 127
31.15	Child, when Herod wakes – 153
31.15	Hush, do not cry, my little tiny child – 152

Ezekiel

3.17	Go, tell it on the mountain – 78

Daniel

7.9	O worship the Lord in the beauty of holiness – 150
12.3	Once in royal David's city – 41

Micah

5.2	Bethlehem, what greater city – 134
5.2	O little town of Bethlehem – 39, 40
5.4	From east to west, from shore to shore – 91

Haggai

2.7	Come, O long-expected Jesus – 2

Malachi

4.2	Hark! the herald angels sing – 84
4.2	Thank you, God, for Mary's child – 182

Matthew

1.21	Mary had a baby – sweet lamb – 48
1.21	Mary had a baby, yes, Lord – 49
1.23	A virgin most holy – 33
1.23	The Lord of life and glory – 155
1.24	As Joseph was awaking – 30, 31
2.1	Angels from the realms of glory – 86
2.1	Hark! do you hear how the angel voices sing – 144
2.1	O leave your sheep – 109

John

1.1	Word of the Father everlasting – 163
1.2	God of God, the uncreated – 75
1.10	He comes to us as one unknown – 167
1.11	Child in the manger – 45
1.12	Christ is born for us today – 52
1.14	Behold, the great Creator makes – 175, 176
1.14	Stars of heaven, clear and bright – 123
1.14	When came in flesh the incarnate Word – 81, 82
1.14	When God from heaven to earth came down – 100
1.17	Christ is the Truth sent from above – 19
1.29	Songs of thankfulness and praise – 161, 162
3.3	Hark! the herald angels sing – 84
4.42	Christians, awake – 118
11.25	Good Christians, all, rejoice – 70
19.2	Child of the stable's secret birth – 46, 47
19.2	Jesus, child of Mary – 124
20.29	No frightened shepherds now – 184

1 Corinthians

1.25	Child in a stable – 35
1.27	Jesus, child of Mary – 124
1.27	Lift your heart and raise your voice – 107
8.9	See him lying on a bed of straw – 110, 111

2 Corinthians

4.6	O slumber, heaven-born treasure – 59
4.6	Silent night! holy night – 80
8.9	Come, see a little tender babe – 37, 38
8.9	In the bleak mid-winter – 42
8.9	Jesus, saviour, holy child – 64
8.9	See him lying on a bed of straw – 110, 111

Ephesians

5.14	Christians, awake – 118
5.14	Wake, O wake, and sleep no longer – 10

Philippians

2.6	Before the heaven and earth – 171, 172
2.6	Down from the height – 173, 174
2.6	How joyful is the song – 179
2.6	The darkness turns to dawn – 21, 22
2.7	Behold, the great Creator makes – 175, 176
2.7	Come and sing the Christmas story – 101
2.7	From east to west, from shore to shore – 91
2.7	Jesus, child of Mary – 124
2.7	Jesus, saviour, holy child – 64
2.7	Not in lordly state and splendour – 44
2.7	Rejoice and sing – 170
2.10	Angels from the realms of glory – 86

Colossians

1.15	Rejoice with heart and voice – 72
1.16	Bow down, you stars – 23
1.16	God of God, the uncreated – 75

1 Thessalonians
    4.16   Hark! a trumpet call is sounding – 12

1 Timothy
    1.15   Good Christians, all, rejoice – 70

Hebrews
    1.3   The darkness turns to dawn – 21, 22
    1.10   Bow down, you stars – 23
    1.10   Creator of the stars of light – 3
    1.10   See amid the winter snow – 119
    4.15   Holy child, how still you lie – 55
    11.10   As with gladness men of old – 146
    12.2   Wake, O wake, and sleep no longer – 10

1 John
    3.5   Songs of thankfulness and praise – 161, 162
    4.9   Had he not loved us – 166
    4.9   Love came down at Christmas – 164, 165

Revelation
    1.7   Lo, he comes with clouds descending – 11
    1.7   We hail the approaching God – 16
    4.6   Wake, O wake, and sleep no longer – 10
    6.12   Songs of thankfulness and praise – 161, 162
    22.16   How brightly gleams the morning star – 135

AUTHORS AND ORIGINATORS

Alexander, Cecil Frances (1818–1895) – 41
Anstice, Joseph (1808–1836) – 81, 82
Baker, Henry Williams (1821–1877) – 75
Baring-Gould, Sabine (1834–1924) – 27, 58
Bartholomew, William (1793–1867) – 24
Bate, Herbert Newell (1871–1941) – 136
Berlioz, Hector (1803–1869) – 151
Black, Brian (born 1926) – 171, 172
Brooks, Phillips (1835–1893) – 39, 40
Byrom, John (1692–1763) – 118
Caird, George Bradford (1917–1984) – 147
Campbell, Robert (1814–1868) – 179
Caswall, Edward (1814–1878) – 12, 119
Cennick, John (1718–1755) – 11
Chandler, John (1806–1876) – 160
Clarkson, Margaret (born 1915) – 15
Coffin, Charles (1676–1749) – 16, 160
Cornelius, Peter (1824–1874) – 136
Croo, Robert (1534) – 152
Davies, John (1787–1855) – 59
Dearmer, Percy (1867–1936) – 181
Dix, William Chatterton (1837–1898) – 133, 146
Doddridge, Philip (1702–1751) – 9, 14
Dudley-Smith, Timothy (born 1926) – 21, 22, 44, 46, 47, 55, 56, 93, 123, 154, 166, 167, 178
Ellerton, John (1826–1893) – 91
Farjeon, Eleanor (1881–1965) – 13
Flechier, E (1632–1710) – 35
Gaunt, Alan (born 1935) – 182
Gerhardt, Paul (1607–1676) – 89, 90
Germanus (c634–732) – 95
Goldschmidt, Otto (1829–1907) – 24
Heber, Reginald (1783–1826) – 140
Hockridge, Kenneth Galsworthy (born 1924) – 155
Hopkins, John Henry (1820–1891) – 139
Hosmer, Frederick Lucian (1840–1929) – 4
Idle, Christopher Martin (born 1938) – 10, 28, 112
Kiddle, Isobel (born 1923) – 23
La Monnoye, Bernard de (1641–1728) – 113
Luther, Martin (1483–1546) – 79
Macbean, Lachlan (1853–1931) – 45
MacDonald, Mary (1789–1872) – 45
Madan, Martin (1726–1790) – 11
McFarland, John (c 1906) – 57
Milton, John (1608–1674) – 7
Möhr, Joseph (1792–1848) – 80

Monsell, John Samuel Bewley (1811–1875) – 150
Montgomery, James (1771–1854) – 86
Morison, John (1750–1798) – 20
Mowbray, David (born 1938) – 8, 158, 163
Murray, Dom Anthony Gregory (born 1916) – 71
Neale, John Mason (1818–1866) – 1, 52, 70, 75, 95, 177, 181
Nicolai, Philipp (1556–1608) – 10
Oakeley, Frederick (1802–1880) – 102
Perry, Michael Arnold (born 1942) – 3, 5, 16, 17, 25, 35, 43, 60, 64, 65, 68, 72, 74, 79, 85, 101, 106, 107, 110, 111, 114, 124, 126, 127, 128, 129, 130, 134, 173, 174
Pestel, Thomas (c1585–1660) – 175, 176
Porteous, Christopher (born 1935) – 54
Prudentius (348–c413) – 75, 134
Reed, Edith Margaret Gellibrand (1885–1933) – 83
Rees, Bryn Austin (1911–1983) – 168
Rossetti, Christina Georgina (1830–1894) – 42, 164, 165
Rutter, John (born 1945) – 109, 144
Santeuil, Jean Baptiste de (1630–1697) – 179
Sargent, Malcolm (1895–1967) – 115
Saward, Michael John (born 1932) – 29, 122
Scheidt, Samuel (1587–1654) – 65
Schlegel, Johann Adolf (1721–1793) – 135
Sears, Edmund Hamilton (1810–1876) – 92
Seddon, James Edward (1915–1983) – 156,157
Sedulius Caelius (died c.450) – 91
Smart, Christopher (1722–1771) – 131, 132
Southwell, Robert (1561–1595) – 37, 38
Tate, Nahum (1652–1715) – 77
Troutbeck, John (1832–1899) – 53, 170
Wade, John Francis (1711–1786) – 102, 103
Ward, Lela Hoover – 112
Watts, Isaac (1674–1748) – 18
Weissel, Georg (1590–1635) – 6
Wesley, Charles (1707–1788) – 2, 11
Wesley, Charles (1707–1788) – and others – 84
Wigmore, Paul (born 1925) – 32, 34, 50, 51, 61, 62, 63, 69, 87, 88, 94, 96, 97, 104, 113, 116, 125, 137, 138, 143, 145, 148, 149, 151, 184
Wilbur, Richard (born 1921) – 36
Winkworth, Catherine (1827–1878) – 6, 89, 90, 135

COMPOSERS, ARRANGERS AND SOURCES OF TUNES

Polish melody – 83, 125, 144
Praetorius, Michael (1571–1621) – 5, 95
Ravenscroft's Psalter (1621) – 14
Rheinhardt, Johann Heinrich (1754) – 150
Robinson, Christopher (born 1935) – 84, 92, 120
Rose, Barry (born 1934) – 13
Routley, Erik Reginald (1917–1982) – 36, 93, 183
Rusbridge, Arthur Ewart (1917–1969) – 83
Russian melody – 114
Sandys, William (1792–1874) – 22, 117
Schulz, Johann Abraham Peter (1747–1800) – 104, 105
Scottish Psalter, Edinburgh (1615) – 20
Shaw, Geoffrey Turton (1879–1943) – 73
Shaw, Martin Edward Fallas (1875–1958) – 15, 163, 174
Smith, Kenneth Donald (born 1928) – 134
Spangenberg, J (1484–1550) – 69
Stainer, John (1840–1901) – 2, 70, 120, 142, 177
Steggall, Charles (1826–1905) – 161
Sullivan, Arthur Seymour (1842–1900) – 92
Swedish melody – 138

Terry, Richard Runciman (1865–1938) – 31
Thrupp, Joseph Francis (1827–1867) – 140
Tochter Zion, Cologne (1741) – 8
Tredinnick, Noël Harwood (born 1949) – 1, 45, 61, 173
Vaughan Williams, Ralph (1872–1958) – 19, 39, 147, 181
Wade, John Francis (1711–1786) – 102
Wainwright, John (1723–1768) – 118
Warlock, Peter (1894–1930) – 71
Warren, Norman Leonard (born 1934) – 21, 28, 38, 47, 114, 124, 126, 131, 167, 182
Welsh melody – 44, 101, 106
Wesley, Samuel Sebastian (1810–1876) – 17
West Indian melody – 48, 49, 121
White, Gilbert Peter (born 1937) – 37, 166
Williams, Aaron (1731–1776) – 16
Wilson, David Gordon (born 1940) – 154, 178
Witt, Christian Friedrich (1660–1716) – 134
Wood, Charles (1866–1926) – 33, 99
Woodward, George Ratcliffe (1848–1934) – 76
Wyton, Alec (born 1921) – 132
Yugoslavian melody – 85

FIRST LINES, TITLES AND SOURCES OF WORDS
ALPHABETICAL INDEX

Italicised lines indicate translations, versions and titles

A child is born in Bethlehem (A child is born) – 126
A child is born in Bethlehem (Sing nowell) – 127
A child this day is born – 117
A great and mighty wonder – 95
A little child there is y-born (Descend from heaven, you angels bright) – 66
A song was heard at Christmas – 178
A stable lamp is lighted – 36
A tender shoot has started – 24
A virgin most holy – 33
A virgin most pure (A virgin most holy) – 33
A virgin unspotted (A virgin most holy) – 33
Adeste fideles laeti triumphantes (O come, all ye faithful) – 102, 103
All my heart this night rejoices (All my heart) – 90
All my heart this night rejoices (Bonn) – 89
All through the night (Come and sing the Christmas story) – 101
Angels from the realms of glory – 86
Angelus ad virginem (Gabriel the angel came) – 25
As Joseph was awaking (Cherry Tree Carol) – 30
As Joseph was awaking (Joseph) – 31
As with gladness men of old – 146
Away in a manger – 57
Before the heaven and earth (Munden) – 171
Before the heaven and earth (Narenza) – 172
Behold, a little tender babe (Come, see a little tender babe) – 37, 38
Behold, the great Creator makes (Kilmarnock) – 175
Behold, the great Creator makes (This endris nyght) – 176
Bellman's Carol (When came in flesh the incarnate Word) – 81, 82
Besançon Carol (Mary, ride on to David's town) – 34
Besançon Carol (People, look east) – 13
Bethlehem, we come to bring – 113
Bethlehem, what greater city – 134
Bow down, you stars – 23
Bright mystical starlight – 137
Brightest and best – 140
Calypso Carol (See him lying on a bed of straw) – 110, 111
Cherry Tree Carol (As Joseph was awaking) – 30, 31
Child in a stable – 35
Child in the manger – 45
Child of heaven born on earth – 43
Child of mine, the Virgin sings – 158
Child of the stable's secret birth (Morwenstow) – 46
Child of the stable's secret birth (Secret Birth) – 47
Child, when Herod wakes – 153
Christ is born for us today – 52
Christ is born within a stable – 114
Christ is the Truth sent from above – 19
Christians, awake – 118

Christians, make a joyful sound – 74
Christmas for God's holy people – 122
Come and hear the joyful singing – 106
Come and sing the Christmas story – 101
Come, O long-expected Jesus – 2
Come, see a little tender babe (Newtown Linford) – 37
Come, see a little tender babe (Peak Hill) – 38
Come, thou long-expected Jesus (Come, O long-expected Jesus) – 2
Come, thou redeemer of the earth (O come, our world's Redeemer, come) – 5
Come to Bethlehem and see the new-born king – 71
Conditor alme siderum (Creator of the stars of light) – 3
Corde natus ex Parentis (God of God, the uncreated) – 75
Coventry Carol (Hush, do not cry) – 152
Creator of the stars of light – 3
Dans cette étable (Child in a stable) – 35
Deck the hall with boughs of holly (Come and hear the joyful singing) – 106
Descend from heaven, you angels bright – 66
Ding-dong, ding (Wake then, Christian, come and listen) – 76
Ding-dong! Merrily on high – 99
Donkey and ox around his bed – 50, 51
Dormi Jesu! Mater ridet (Sleep, Lord Jesus!) – 60
Down from the height (Purpose) – 173
Down from the height (Slane) – 174
Earth has many a noble city (Bethlehem, what greater city) – 134
Echo Carol (From highest heaven where praises ring) – 79
Entre le boeuf et l'âne gris (Donkey and ox around his bed) – 50, 51
Es ist ein' Ros' (A great and mighty wonder) – 95
Es wird scho glei dumpa (The daylight is fading) – 62
Et barn er født i Betlehem (A child is born in Bethlehem) – 126, 127
Every star shall sing a carol (Christmas for God's holy people) – 122
Faithful vigil ended – 154
Fragrance (Word of the Father everlasting) – 163
Freut euch und singt (Rejoice and sing) – 170
Fröhlich soll mein Herze springen (All my heart this night rejoices) – 89, 90
From east to west, from shore to shore – 91
From highest heaven where praises ring – 79
Gabriel's Message (The angel Gabriel from heaven came) – 27
Gabriel the angel came – 25
Gallery Carol (Rejoice and be merry) – 141
Gaudete, gaudete, Christus est natus (Rejoice with heart and voice) – 72
Geborn ist uns ein Kindelein (Travellers all to Bethlehem) – 69
Girls and boys, leave your toys – 115
Glad music fills the Christmas sky – 68
Go, tell it on the mountain – 78
God is in Bethlehem (God to Adam came in Eden) – 97
God of God, the uncreated – 75
God rest you merry, gentlemen – 120
God to Adam came in Eden – 97
Good Christian men, rejoice (Good Christians, all, rejoice) – 70
Good Christians, all, rejoice – 70
Good King Wenceslas looked out – 177
Had he not loved us – 166
Hajej, nynej (Jesus, saviour, holy child) – 64
Hark, a thrilling voice is sounding (Hark! a trumpet call is sounding) – 12
Hark! a trumpet call is sounding – 12
Hark! do you hear how the angel voices sing – 144
Hark the glad sound – 14
Hark! the herald angels sing – 84
He comes to us as one unknown – 167
Hear the skies around – 85
He is born, the king divine (Child of heaven born on earth) – 43
Holy child, how still you lie (Holy child) – 56

Holy child, how still you lie (Ruxley) – 55
Holy, joyful dawn of Christmas – 94
How brightly gleams the morning star – 135
How joyful is the song – 179
Hush, do not cry, my little tiny child – 152
I heard a mother tenderly sing – 67
I himmelen, I himmelen (The star of heaven foretells) – 138
I saw a fair maiden sitten and sing (I heard a mother tenderly sing) – 67
I saw my love by lantern light – 61
I saw three ships (When God from heaven to earth came down) – 100
I see your crib – 54
I wonder as I wander – 169
Ihr Kinderlein kommet (O come, all you children) – 104, 105
Il est né le divin enfant (Child of heaven born on earth) – 43
Il s'en va loin de la terre (Jesus, child of gentle Mary) – 151
In dieser armen Krippe liegt (Within this humble manger lies) – 53
In dulci jubilo (Good Christians, all, rejoice) – 70
In the bleak mid-winter – 42
Infant holy, infant lowly – 83
Instantis adventum Dei (We hail the approaching God) – 16
It came upon the midnight clear – 92
Jesus, child of gentle Mary – 151
Jesus, child of Mary – 124
Jesus Christ the Lord is born – 130
Jesus, good above all other – 181
Jesus, hope of every nation – 17
Jesus noster Jesus bonus (Jesus, good above all other) – 181
Jesus, saviour, holy child – 64
Jesus the saviour comes – 15
Jesus, you are welcome – 145
Jezus malusienki (Such a night in Bethlehem) – 125
Jordans orus praeria (On Jordan's bank the Baptist's cry) – 160
Joseph was an old man (As Joseph was awaking) – 30, 31
Joy to the world! The Lord has come – 18
Lift up your heads, you mighty gates – 6
Lift your heart and raise your voice – 107
Little children, wake and listen – 112
Little Jesus, sweetly sleep (Jesus, saviour, holy child) – 64
Lo, he comes with clouds descending – 11
Lord, now let your servant (Caswall) – 157
Lord, now let your servant (North Coates) – 156
Love came down at Christmas (Gartan) – 164
Love came down at Christmas (Hermitage) – 165
Love is come again (Mary came with meekness) – 143
Lullay, lullay, thou little tiny child (Hush, do not cry) – 152
Lullay my liking (I heard a mother tenderly sing) – 67
Magnificat (My soul proclaims the greatness of the Lord) – 28
Magnificat (Now sing my soul, 'How great the Lord!') – 29
Mary came with meekness – 143
Mary had a baby – sweet lamb – 48
Mary had a baby, yes, Lord – 49
Mary, ride on to David's town – 34
Mega kai paradoxa thauma (A great and mighty wonder) – 95
My soul proclaims the greatness of the Lord – 28
Nesem vam noviny (Softly, a shepherd is singing his song) – 88
No frightened shepherds now – 184
No small wonder (Small wonder the star) – 148, 149
Noël nouvelet (Mary came with meekness) – 143
Nos Galan (Come and hear the joyful singing) – 106
Not in lordly state and splendour – 44
Now sing my soul, 'How great the Lord!' – 29
Now the green blade riseth (Mary came with meekness) – 143

Song of Christ's Glory (Jesus, hope of every nation) – 17
Song of Mary (My soul proclaims the greatness of the Lord) – 28
Song of Mary (Now sing my soul, 'How great the Lord!') – 29
Song of Simeon (Faithful vigil ended) – 154
Song of Simeon (Lord, now let your servant) – 156, 157
Songs of thankfulness and praise (St Edmund) – 161
Songs of thankfulness and praise (St George's, Windsor) – 162
Stars of heaven clear and bright – 123
Still, still, still – 96
Stille Nacht! heilige Nacht (Silent night! holy night) – 80
Stranger in Bethlehem (To Bethlehem the strangers came) – 32
Such a night in Bethlehem – 125
Susanni (Descend from heaven, you angels bright) – 66
Sussex Carol (On Christmas night all Christians sing) – 98
Take God's good news to saddened hearts – 8
Thank you God for Mary's child – 182
The advent of our King (We hail the approaching God) – 16
The angel Gabriel from heaven came – 27
The angels and the shepherds (Softly, a shepherd is singing) – 87, 88
The darkness turns to dawn (Saigon) – 21
The darkness turns to dawn (Sandys) – 22
The daylight is fading – 62, 63
The first nowell – 142
The God we seek – 168
The holly and the ivy – 159
The Lord of life and glory – 155
The Lord will come and not be slow – 7
The moon shines bright (When came in flesh the incarnate Word) – 81
The people who in darkness walked – 20
The star of heaven foretells – 138
The truth from above (Christ is the Truth sent from above) – 19
The virgin Mary had a baby boy – 121
There's a saviour to see – 108
This endris nyght I saw a sight (Behold, the great Creator makes) – 176
This endris nyght I saw a sight (From east to west, from shore to shore) – 91
This is the Truth sent from above (Christ is the Truth sent from above) – 19
Thou didst leave thy holy dwelling (Jesus, child of gentle Mary) – 151
Thou whom shepherds worshipped hearing (Shepherds came) – 147
Three kings from Persian lands afar – 136
Thy kingdom come! On bended knee (Your kingdom come) – 4
To Bethlehem the strangers came – 32
To us in Bethlem city (The Lord of life and glory) – 155
Travellers all to Bethlehem – 69
Uns ist geborn ein Kindelein (Jesus Christ the Lord is born) – 130
Unto us a boy is born (Jesus Christ the Lord is born) – 130
Up, good Christen folk and listen (Wake then, Christian, come and listen) – 76
Veni, Redemptor gentium (O come, our world's Redeemer, come) – 5
Veni, veni Emmanuel (O come, O come, Emmanuel) – 1
Vom Himmel hoch (From highest heaven where praises ring) – 79
Vox clara ecce intonat (Hark! a trumpet call is sounding) – 12
W zlobie lezy (Infant holy, infant lowly) – 83
Wachet auf, ruft uns die Stimme (Wake, O wake, and sleep no longer) – 10
Wake, O wake, and sleep no longer – 10
Wake then, Christian, come and listen – 76
We hail the approaching God – 16
We three kings of Orient are – 139
What Child is this – 133
When came in flesh the incarnate Word (Bellman's Carol) – 81
When came in flesh the incarnate Word (St Stephen) – 82
When God from heaven to earth came down – 100
When the angel came to Mary – 26
Where is this stupendous stranger (Kit Smart) – 132